No Nonsense
PRINCE2™

Accredited Pre-Course Reading

Key facts and cross topic
themes, with a little help
from the Romans!

By Charles Fox
Sketches by Wyn Johnson

Preface

The author of this book has spent two decades trying to be a better project manager, most of it making slow progress. If he ever succeeds, he is going to write a book about it. In the meantime you'll have to make do with this one. Charles Fox has worked in PRINCE2™ (P2) project environments, and its predecessors, for about 18 years. He has seen many personal and business benefits from adopting good project management practices. There have even been a few days when he has gone home on time, and none of his customers want to sue him at the moment.

For the last 10 years Charles has been coaching others in good project management practices, and he is an Accredited PRINCE2™ (P2) Trainer and consultant. Charles has a talent for explaining complicated things in simple ways, and after constant nagging by training course delegates and customers, decided to write a no nonsense explanation of the value of the P2 structured project management method and the key facts from the official manual. This book is *not* a replacement for the official PRINCE2™ (P2) manual – it is an outline of the key facts, and a brief explanation of why P2 can be so useful in change management.

Charles lives in deepest darkest Wiltshire with his wife, children and a Triumph Bonneville that looks nice but refuses to stop leaking oil. People say he is surprisingly old, and a surprisingly poor motorcycle mechanic.

Charles Fox

No Nonsense
PRINCE2™

Published by Core IS Ltd
V3.5

Reviewed by
Bruce Aitken, Stephen Barney, Joyce Brook, Jim Gilhooley

Foreword

I wrote this book because a steady stream of people said I should. Friends, clients and training course delegates told me that I had a talent for explaining the complex P2 method in a straightforward way, shrinking the official 457 page manual down to the key facts that you need to know to understand how P2 works. When I asked a few more people what information they wanted, they said there was a need to describe, in a no nonsense way, how the timeline and key cross-topic themes work in P2.

I was standing in a train at 6:30am one grey Monday morning (en route to deliver a P2 training course), thinking about a relative with cancer and wondering how I could help. I decided that if I wrote a book about P2 I would dedicate a proportion of any income to help people with cancer. I started making some notes. By the end of the week I had written half the book. (There were a lot of train delays that week). The other half of the book took another six months.

I decided to use images of the Romans to illustrate some of the key points from P2 and to provide some light relief. (The Romans, so far as I am aware, are not role models for adoption of P2 – they're just there to liven things up a bit).

For me, the value of P2 is in encouraging people to be more effective by being more results focussed. I hope this book helps you discover how P2 can help you.

Postscript
Since writing this book my good friend and colleague, David Allcorn, was diagnosed with cancer and died in December 2004. He was so much more than just an accountant. His departure has left me feeling angry that this disease can cut down our loved ones so indiscriminately. I am told that cancer will affect 25% of us at some point in our lifetimes; that's 25% of the readers of this book, 25% of our families, 25% of our friends, 25% of our colleagues. Please do whatever you can to help cancer charities find a cure. If you would like to help or make a donation see www.cancerresearchuk.org or contact the author at www.coreis.co.uk .

At least £1 will be given to a cancer research or cancer care charity for every copy of this book.
Thank you for your contribution.

Contents

Chapter 1.   How to use this Book

What is *No Nonsense PRINCE2?*
PRINCE2 (P2) is a project management method – a set of guiding principles and scaleable process steps for managing any size or shape of project. P2 is defined in a manual called *Managing Successful Projects with PRINCE2*. Many organisations have tailored and adopted aspects of P2 to foster results-orientated work by their staff. Internationally recognised *Foundation* and *Practitioner* qualifications in the method are becoming increasingly important in job markets.

The PRINCE2 manual is an extensive reference book. It is not designed solely as a learning tool. It includes much valuable supporting information, templates and advice on implementation that can get in the way of discovering the basic key facts about what this project management method actually is.

The purpose of *No Nonsense PRINCE2* is to state the facts about:

- ❏   what PRINCE2 is and how it is structured
- ❏   how each of the separate modules work
- ❏   how key cross-topic themes work
- ❏   how the timeline works.

Having got your head around the basic facts, you can then proceed to the official manual for the full depth and supporting material.

Which chapters should you read?
No Nonsense PRINCE2 distills the key facts from the official manual, and is a good starting point for understanding the method and the key facts. Serious users of P2, and Practitioner examination candidates, will need to refer to the formal manual for finer detail, document templates and advice on implementation.

The bulk of *No Nonsense PRINCE2* is structured in the same way as the official manual, describing the 19 Components, Processes and Techniques one module at a time within 3 major sections. Each major section is prefaced with a *One Minute Overview* for anyone wanting a really fast, high caffeine introduction.

Chapter 2 provides essential background on what P2 is and why people are finding it so valuable.

Chapter 3 describes each of the 8 P2 Components.

Chapter 4 describes each of the 8 P2 Processes and the 45 sub-processes within them.

Chapter 5 describes the 3 P2 Techniques.

Chapter 6 describes key cross-topic themes that are very fragmented in the P2 manual. Information from chapters 3,4 and 5 are woven together to explain how themes like Exception Handling work.

Chapter 6 also includes a walk down the timeline, describing a fictitious project that illustrates how P2 works over time. This will help readers understand how the different parts of P2 link together throughout the project life cycle.

Chapter 7 gives hints and tips on passing the Foundation and Practitioner exams.

The P2 FISH diagram is a visual time line showing the interaction between the 8 processes, plus when the key documents and other deliverables are produced. If you are lost in the detail of P2, don't get into a flap, just check where you are against the fish.

If you are new to P2
If you have not been introduced to P2 and its' terminology before, I suggest you read *No Nonsense PRINCE2* from the start to finish, but don't worry about details too much – just get the flavour of each chapter. Having got an overview of all of P2 and how it works, you can then go back and investigate individual modules in more detail.

More experienced readers
If you are already familiar with the basic concepts and the terminology, I suggest you pick and choose from the chapters you are interested in. Chapter 6 describes important key cross-topic themes that are rather fragmented in the official manual.

Exam Candidates
No Nonsense PRINCE2 can help exam candidates by revealing the key facts from the official manual and explaining how it all works. However, the official PRINCE2 manual is your ultimate reference.

No Nonsense PRINCE2 provides most of the details necessary to pass the multiple choice Foundation exam, provided that you understand and memorise them. The Foundation exam is closed book – brains only! Concentrate on the terminology used, and the 'Phrases to Remember' section of each chapter.

Practitioner exam candidates may find Chapter 6 useful as it explains important cross-topic themes that are fragmented in the official manual. You can take paper versions of *No Nonsense PRINCE2* into the Practitioner exam and refer to it, however electronic versions are not allowed in the exam room.

Feedback
If you have any feedback on *No Nonsense PRINCE2* please email it to info@coreis.co.uk or contact Core IS Ltd.

Chapter 2.   Essential Background

2.1.   What is PRINCE2?

PRINCE2 is an approach to management that describes how to make changes to product lines, services or some other aspect of the host organisation in an effective way. It encourages the following at management and specialist team levels:

- ❑ clarity of purpose
- ❑ avoidance of muddle
- ❑ minimum surprises.

The PRINCE2 method is defined within a 457 page encyclopaedia-like manual that describes 19 different aspects of good change management practices one module at a time, plus extensive appendices. The focus of is upon:

- ❑ key components that should be managed with care whilst implementing change
- ❑ procedural steps to take at different times whilst implementing change
- ❑ some useful day to day techniques.

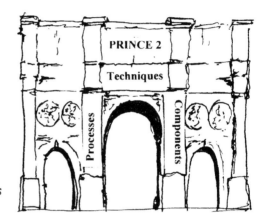

The method advocates a project based approach to management of change. This means:

- ❑ defining what must be changed and why
- ❑ setting up temporary roles and responsibilities for people involved in implementing the change
- ❑ planning, resourcing and management of the activities required to bring about change.

PRINCE2 is very flexible. It can be tailored to work in:

- ❑ any culture
- ❑ any type or size of project
- ❑ any degree of formality
- ❑ any type of change.

The PRINCE2 method is owned and promoted by the Office of Government Commerce (OGC, part of the UK Treasury). The PRINCE2 manual is Crown Copyright, however anybody may use the method without fees or royalties. Although originally aimed at the public sector, it is now being adopted faster in the private sector and is growing in importance internationally.

P2 is increasingly being recognised as the standard for effective organisation of change, and is being adopted by management bodies as a measure of management skill. Internationally recognised examinations are available to demonstrate proof of an individuals' mastery of the method. Examinations, trainers and consultants are administered by the APM Group Ltd, who ensure that high standards are consistently maintained globally.

People sometimes say that P2 is bureaucratic and involves too much paper. This is a misunderstanding. The vast majority of the method is highly tailorable and can easily be merged with different working cultures. The 'documents' referred to in the method are just sets of information, they do not need to be on paper at all. Poor implementations can be bureaucratic and excessively paper based, however the method itself is not. The PRINCE2 manual contains *extensive description* rather than *excessive prescription*.

The Structure of PRINCE2

The method is structured in a similar way to a recipe for an apple pie! Major sections in the manual are:

- ❏ Components
  Equivalent to the ingredients of a pie.

- ❏ Processes
  Equivalent to the steps required to make a pie from the ingredients.

- ❏ Techniques
  Equivalent to the skills needed to be able to process the ingredients.

The 8 Components

These are like the list of ingredients needed for an apple pie. Each ingredient is described in terms of why it is needed and it's key characteristics. Apples are one of the key components of an apple pie; the best apple pies use good apples rather than bad ones. The best projects use good versions of the PRINCE2 components.

The method describes 8 components:

1. The Business Case
Reasons for the project plus an investment appraisal. Used as the basis for all management decisions.
2. Organisation
Roles and responsibilities of people in projects.
3. Controls
Governance arrangements such as reporting, escalation procedures and decision making authority.
4. Quality in a Project Environment
How to set and then meet expectations for characteristics of deliverables and the final outcome of the project.

5. Plans
Definitions of the Products (deliverables) required, and the detail of the activities needed to construct them.
6. Risk Management
Control of threats to success that might undermine the Business Case unless managed.
7. Change Control
Ensuring that only beneficial changes to previous agreements are implemented.
8. Configuration Management
Tracking of deliverables, control and distribution of changing versions of key deliverables.

The 8 Processes
These are like the steps that are needed to construct an apple pie from the components. (E.G. first peel and slice the apples, then put them in the pie dish, and lastly put the pastry on top.) All processes are scaleable in terms of size and formality. Some PRINCE2 processes are sequential others operate in parallel.

The method describes 8 processes:

1. Starting Up a Project (SU) process
Pre-project preparation, high-level early analysis of the project, appointment of the decision making team.
2. Initiating a Project (IP) process
Mandatory definition of as much of the project as is visible at the time, before commencement of hands-on activities to construct deliverables.
3. Directing a Project (DP) process
The work of the Project Board members.
4. Controlling a Stage (CS) process
The day to day work of the Project Manager between formal assessments by the Project Board.
5. Managing Product Delivery (MP) process
The day to day work of the Team Managers between formal assessments by the Project Board.
6. Managing Stage Boundaries (SB) process
The work of the Project Manager in preparing for a formal assessment by the Project Board.
7. Planning (PL) process
A series of steps used to construct a Plan. The Planning process is used at various points throughout a project.
8. Closing a Project (CP) process
Orderly close down, handover and review.

The 3 Techniques
Creating a good apple pie requires mastery of a set of techniques such as peeling apples and rolling pastry. Creating a good project outcome also requires mastery of many techniques, some of which are described in P2.

The method describes 3 techniques:

1. Product Based Planning technique
A powerful visual technique for:
❑ visually identifying hierarchical families of deliverables that the project must create
❑ negotiating the quality criteria for each deliverable so that users know what to expect, and suppliers know what to create
❑ visually working out the optimum logical relationships between deliverables as a stepping stone to producing the optimum Plan of activities.

2. Change Control technique
A technique for processing Change Requests in the same way as Project Issues.

3. Quality Review technique
A technique for reviewing allegedly completed deliverables (to see if they meet previously agreed quality criteria), without having unnecessary meetings.

2.2. Why bother with PRINCE2?
The adoption of PRINCE2 is accelerating rapidly in both public and private sectors because people are finding real world benefits from using it:

❑ Benefits to senior management
- greater predictability in management of change
- direct link between strategic objectives and operational change
- encourages effective working at all levels
- fact based business decisions
- resources committed in Stages
- clarity of what will be achieved if resources are committed
- clarity of whether a target is achievable
- immediate escalation if business benefits are threatened
- control without bureaucracy
- dramatically reduced time in meetings
- compliance to established best practice.

❑ Benefits to Project Managers
- internationally recognised UKAS accredited qualifications
- career development
- improved leadership and delegation framework
- fewer meetings
- clarity of what has to be delivered
- more time to focus on high value activities like risk management
- don't have to be a technical specialist to run a technical project
- one set of principles that can be applied to any size of project in any environment.

❑ Benefits to Teams
- fewer meetings and less report writing
- freedom to work in their own way
- clear expectations for what to deliver, when and why
- user's quality criteria for finished deliverables agreed BEFORE commencement of activity planning
- opportunity to negotiate key dates and details with Project Manager and users before work commences
- involvement in decisions about change requests
- clear decision making authority and escalation procedures
- opportunities for linking team delivery to personal objectives.

2.3. What is NOT in PRINCE2?

The method does not attempt to define everything needed in either the 'perfect' project or the 'perfect' project person, since these are adequately defined elsewhere.

Notable exclusions from the method are:

❑ soft skills such as motivation, leadership and negotiation
❑ financial management, contracts and procurement
❑ tools such as estimating or planning tools.

Although soft skills are not described within the method, it does include many of the essential aspects of strong leadership, such as definition of what others must do, control systems and delegation mechanisms.

2.4. When NOT to use PRINCE2

PRINCE2 is not suitable for every situation. In particular it is not suitable when:

❑ there is no desire (or need) to be results oriented or have effective working practices
❑ the objectives of change are not clear
❑ the key deliverables are not yet clear enough to be outlined in the early stages of a project.

In the latter two cases the Managing Successful Programmes (MSP) method (also from OGC) should be used rather than PRINCE2. MSP focuses on mastering uncertainty so that the right projects are identified and then run at the right time. The focus of PRINCE2 is to then run the project in the right way so that a specific objective is achieved.

Phrases to Remember

a) P2 project managers are able to:

- establish terms of reference as a prerequisite to the start of a project
- use a defined structure for delegation, authority and communication
- divide the project in manageable stages for better planning and control
- ensure resource commitment from management is part of any approval to proceed
- provide regular, but brief, management reports
- keep meetings short, timely and relevant.

b) P2 covers the project lifecycle and some pre-project preparation.

c) P2 can be used in any environment for any size of project.

d) Tailoring is critical to successful adoption of the method.

e) P2 is considered to be *process based*.

Chapter 3.   The 8 PRINCE2 Components

3.1.   One Minute Overview

The 8 P2 Components are analogous to the ingredients of an apple pie. If apples, flour, water etc are carefully selected, prepared and then mixed together in the right way, they will be transformed into a beautiful apple pie. Similarly, if the P2 Components are prepared properly and then mixed together in the way described by the P2 processes, the project will be much more likely to succeed.

The 8 Components are:

- **The Business Case**
  The set of reasons that justify the project or prove that it should not be run any further.
- **Organisation**
  PRINCE2 includes standard roles that must be tailored and resourced to suit local needs.
- **Controls**
  Governance mechanisms that allow the project to be started, run, changed and closed in a non bureaucratic yet controlled way.
- **Quality**
  Setting and then meeting expectations for how the project will produce the right deliverables.
- **Plans**
  Definitions of what the project will produce, how, at what cost and over what time period.
- **Risk Management**
  Ensuring that the project takes neither too much nor too little risk, so that the Business Case comes true.
- **Change Control**
  Control of the inevitable changes to previously agreed aspects of the project, so that the change is beneficial.
- **Configuration Management**
  Control of multiple versions of deliverables, key project documents, audit trails of change and archiving.

All components must be tailored to fit local working practices and to meet the needs of each project.

3.2. The Business Case

What's it all about?

The Business Case contains reasons for a project, benefits which will occur if the project finishes successfully, investment appraisal, options, costs, timescales and key risks that would stop the project being successful.

Why bother?

The Business Case states the facts used to decide whether:

- ❑ a project is worth running
- ❑ a project should continue to the next Stage
- ❑ the benefits exceed the risks
- ❑ the investment in the project is justified
- ❑ there is a better way to achieve the same outcome
- ❑ the impact of change requests is acceptable in business terms.

Key Facts

The Business Case may be created before the project starts, following previous research, feasibility studies or programme activity, and given to the project as part of the Project Mandate.

An Outline Business Case is created during Starting up a Project (SU) process, and forms part of the high level outline information the Project Board reviews in Authorising Initiation (DP1) when deciding whether the project is a good enough idea to be worth planning in greater detail.

Any information available at the end of Starting up a Project (SU) process is expanded during Initiating a Project (IP) process. A detailed Business Case is developed in Refining the Business Case and Risks (IP3) based upon any new information and detailed costs, benefits and risks taken from the Project Plan and Stage Plans. This detailed Business Case is part of the Project Initiation Document (PID) that the Project Board reviews in Authorising a Project (DP2) when deciding whether the project should proceed or not.

Towards the end of each Stage, the Business Case is updated in Managing Stage Boundaries process (SB3 Updating a Project Business Case) based on updated information in the Project Plan, next Stage Plan and Risk Log.

Phrases to Remember

a) The set of information that justifies why the project is being started, continued, changed or stopped.
b) Plans provide the time and cost data needed for investment analysis within the Business Case.
c) The Business Case must be updated if Plans or risks change.

3.3. Organisation

What's it all about?
This part of the method defines standard roles that exist in every P2 project, plus the principles behind them. It defines the project organisation chart, roles, responsibilities, and levels of decision making authority.

Why bother?
Good organisation is essential because:

- ❏ organisation is the basis of delegation and control
- ❏ every project will have people in it
- ❏ stakeholders need to have a voice
- ❏ it provides an interface between the outside world, the project manager and teams
- ❏ combined with sensible use of Controls, good application of P2 Organisation can cut out a lot of meetings.

Key Facts
The Project Mandate that triggered SU may include information about key people and stakeholders.

The whole of the Project Organisation Structure is designed and appointed during the Starting up a Project (SU) process. It can be revised at any time, however at the very least should be reviewed during Managing Stage Boundaries (SB) process because it may need to change from Stage to Stage.

Reporting lines:

- ❏ the Project Board reports to corporate or programme management
- ❏ the Project Manager reports to the Project Board
- ❏ the Team Manager(s) report to the Project Manager.

The Project Board
The Project Board consists of 3 interests at all times (Business, User and Supplier). Project Board members should be suitably empowered managers able to make decisions and commit resources. Since they are usually very busy people, Project Board members may delegate some of their duties (especially Project Assurance), however they must NOT delegate their decision making duties.

Project Board Role - The Project Executive
- ❏ is ultimately responsible for the project
- ❏ owns the Business Case
- ❏ is appointed by the host organisation.

Project Board Role - The Senior User(s)
- ❑ represent users at management decision making level
- ❑ are responsible for requirements and user resources
- ❑ is often a marketing manager in cases where there is no direct contact with end users.

Project Board Role - The Senior Supplier(s)
- ❑ represent suppliers of project resources at management decision making level
- ❑ are responsible for viability of any technical/specialist work
- ❑ could include a manager of a third party that is supplying a resource into the project (e.g. the manager of a third party company supplying a software development team)
- ❑ could include in-house managers supplying resources into the project (e.g. the manager of a testing team).

Project Board Role – Project Assurance from User & Business & Supplier perspectives
- ❑ all Project Board members must do (or delegate) Project Assurance
- ❑ to assure themselves that the Plans, Business Case and risks are realistic
- ❑ provides a sanity check for busy Project Board members
- ❑ provide wisdom, experience and advice on day to day matters to the Project Manager and Team Manager(s).

The Project Manager
The Project Manager is responsible for day to day control of a project, and executes a previously agreed Plan, within a Tolerance previously agreed with the Project Board.

There must only be one Project Manager, and they must NOT do Project Assurance. In small projects the Project Manager is often a Team Manager too.

Team Manager(s)
Team Managers represent each team and agree work with the Project Manager through the mechanism of Work Packages. Team membership is outside of PRINCE2 because teams are frequently highly specialised.

Project Support
Project Support people can provide expertise and leg power to help with management of teams and the project as a whole. As well as administrative support, a Project Support service might include highly skilled people such as lawyers, procurement experts, recruitment, planning tool experts, accountants etc.

Phrases to Remember

a) P2 defines roles NOT jobs, all of which must be filled in some way in every project.

b) Roles may be combined, split, shared or delegated in any way subject to three rules:

    Rule 1. only one Project Manager

    Rule 2. the Project Board may not delegate decision making duties

    Rule 3. the Project Manager may not do Project Assurance.

c) Project Assurance can advise on anything, Project Support can help.

d) The Project Board is the voice to the outside world.

3.4. Controls

What's it all about?

PRINCE2 Controls are a bit like the controls of a car – a collection of different things that, taken together, allow the driver to get from A to B and react to events in a sensible way. Controls allow the project to be started up, controlled, steered, monitored and stopped in a controlled way. There are various types of Control, e.g. reports, decision making events, plans, delegation techniques.

There are many different Controls, each of which has a different purpose. Different roles use different Controls. Only 2 Controls (Checkpoint Reports and Highlight Reports) are used on a regular time basis. The rest (like the brakes of a car), are only used when you need them.

Why bother?

If you don't control your car it will not take you to where you plan to go. If you don't have controls in a project, it will not deliver what's in the plan.

Controls ensure that:

- ❏ the project is beneficial (otherwise it gets stopped)
- ❏ the Plans are realistic and achievable
- ❏ teams and suppliers do the right thing
- ❏ expectations for quality are set and then met
- ❏ reporting is timely and effective
- ❏ serious problems and change requests are handled effectively.

The P2 method has a standard list of Controls, however each project must decide which ones are appropriate and how they will be implemented.

Key Facts

Initial expectations for the formality of control and governance may be identified in the Project Mandate, and/or expanded on within the Project Brief created in Starting Up a Project (SU) process. Controls and governance arrangements tend to be very similar from one project to the next in a particular host organisation, so many new projects are able to just pick up existing working practices.

During the Initiating a Project (IP) process, the Controls to be used are defined in detail and documented in the Project Initiation Document (PID). The Project Board will be asked to approve and commit to these Controls at their Authorising a Project (DP2) assessment at the end of IP. Controls may need to change from Stage to Stage according to what is required.

PRINCE2 is designed to encourage *management by exception*, a way of working in which the roles and decision making authority of people is agreed, and escalation rules established. This allows people to work in their own way, as long as:

- ❑ they deliver what was agreed
- ❑ they escalate as soon as they believe Tolerance will not be met
- ❑ they provide regular reports to management.

Controls used when commencing a project:
- ❑ **Project Start-up**
  Setting up a sensible Project Board, and confirming the Project Mandate by producing a Project Brief.
- ❑ **Authorising Initiation (DP1)**
  The Project Board confirm the project looks sensible before investing in the effort of detailed planning that is done (or not as the case may be) in IP.
- ❑ **Project Initiation**
  Detailed planning and project definition leading to assembly of the Project Initiation Document (PID). Once approved, the PID is like a contract between Project Manager, Project Executive, Senior Supplier(s) and Senior User(s) stating what the project will deliver, and how it will be run.
- ❑ **Communications Plan**
  An agreement stating what information will be sent, to whom, when, why, in what format, and how feedback systems will work.
- ❑ **Stage Selection**
  Stages are time partitions of the project bounded by management decision points, e.g. the time between End Stage Assessments during which the Project Manager is executing a previously agreed Stage Plan. Stage length is a key decision based on:
  - level of risk (riskier Stages should be shorter)
  - visibility of the future
  - ability of the Project Board to commit resources to the next Stage Plan. (If they cannot commit the resources needed then the Stage is too long).
- ❑ **Authorising a Project (DP2)**
  At the end of IP the Project Board has the opportunity to review the proposed Plans against the Business Case and Risks. The Project Initiation Document (PID) assembled by the Project Manager in IP6 contains both the Plans and the proposed procedures and processes that will be used by the project. The Project Board should not approve further work on the project unless the Business Case is still valid and the contents of the PID are appropriate.

Controls used in the 'doing' part of a project:
- ❑ **Tolerance**
  Permissible deviation from a previously agreed Plan (or Work Package) without having to refer to a higher authority for approval. Tolerance can be expressed in terms of time, cost, scope, quality, risk or benefit. Riskier Stages should have smaller Tolerance. Tolerance exists at all 4 levels of role defined in PRINCE2.
- ❑ **Product Descriptions**
  Definitions of what a Product is, who will accept it and what quality criteria it must meet.
- ❑ **Work Package Authorisation**
  Work Packages are the only way to agree work with a team or supplier.

- ❏ **Quality Log**
  The Quality Log holds information about expected and actual quality checking activities, extracted from the various Plans into a single log. This makes progress checking, reporting and audit easy, and provides a focus for ensuring that Products are created that meet their previously defined Product Descriptions.
- ❏ **Quality Control**
  Ensuring that a Product meets its' previously agreed quality criteria as defined in its' Product Description.
- ❏ **Project Issues and Change Control**
  Handling of significant problems and Change Requests so that the Plans and Business Case are not undermined.
- ❏ **Risk Log**
  The Risk Log stores results of Risk Analysis, in particular the countermeasures needed to prevent serious risks undermining the Plans and Business Case.
- ❏ **Checkpoints and Checkpoint Reports**
  Checkpoints are an opportunity for Team Managers to assess their progress. Checkpoint Reports are periodic reports from Team Manager to Project Manager advising of progress and problems.
- ❏ **Planning and Re-planning**
  Ensuring that activities are planned so that the required Products are produced in the optimum way.
- ❏ **Daily Log**
  A notepad/diary to help the Project Manager keep track of day to day events without excessive reliance on memory.
- ❏ **Highlight Reports**
  A periodic report from Project Manager to Project Board advising of progress and problems.
- ❏ **End Stage Report**
  A report from Project Manager to Project Board at an End Stage Assessment, summarising the current Stage and making recommendations for the next.
- ❏ **End Stage Assessments (DP3)**
  A formal review of past, present and future by the Project Board. The project does not continue unless the Business Case is valid and they allocate resources required to complete the next Stage Plan.
- ❏ **Exception Report**
  An urgent report from Project Manager to Project Board written as soon as the Project Manager starts to forecast that the current Stage or project will not complete within the previously agreed Tolerance.
- ❏ **Exception Assessment (DP3)**
  A formal review of an Exception Plan by the Project Board; just like a normal End Stage Assessment except it happens in exceptional circumstances.
- ❏ **Lessons Learned Log**
  A log containing information about any lessons learned during a stage. It is particularly useful for helping to improve project management processes, and should be summarised (as minimum) to the Project Board during Managing Stage Boundaries (SB) process.

Controls used at the end of a project:
- ❑ **Project Closure Notification**
  Controlled release of resources when the project has been proved to be finished.
- ❑ **Lessons Learned Report**
  Summary of lessons learned in the project, so that the Project Board can share these experiences outside the project team.
- ❑ **Follow-on Action Recommendations**
  Recommendations for further work *after* the project has ended. E.G. risk management actions, unresolved Project Issues, beneficial Change Requests that have not yet been implemented.
- ❑ **End Project Report**
  A review of the whole project comparing the initial version of the PID with actual events, including review of any benefits visible at that time.

Controls used *after* the end of a project:
- ❑ **Post Project Review**
  A review of the benefits and Business Case for the project, which is organised by the Project Board to take place some time after the project has finished.

Phrases to Remember

a) Stages are time partitions of the project with management decision points.
b) Tolerance is permissible deviation from a Plan without reference to a higher authority. It works at 3 levels:
- ❑ business management to Project Board via the Project Mandate
- ❑ from Project Board to Project Manager via the Project Plan and any Stage Plans
- ❑ from Project Manager to Team Manager(s) via Work Packages.
c) Tolerance is often expressed in terms of permissible percentage time and cost variation, however there are 6 types of Tolerance defined in PRINCE2 – Time, Cost, Scope, Quality, Risk and Benefit.
- ❑ time – e.g. finish on March 30th plus or minus 1 week
- ❑ cost – e.g. finish the Stage at planned cost plus or minus 5%
- ❑ scope – e.g. maximise the specification but do not exceed cost
- ❑ quality – e.g. finish the Product as quickly as possible however there must be no serious defects
- ❑ risk – e.g. escalate immediately if any new high impact risks are identified
- ❑ benefit – e.g. escalate immediately if the project is expected to increase company profits by more than 2%.
d) Exception handling is invoked as soon as the Project Manager forecasts that the current Stage or the whole project cannot be completed within the Tolerance previously agreed with the Project Board.
e) Long Work Packages should be split at Stage boundaries so that there is visibility of progress at the End Stage Assessment by the Project Board.
f) Checkpoint Reports are from Team Manager to Project Manager.

g) Reports from the Project Manager to the Project Board are:
- Highlight Report (at regular intervals)
- End Stage Report (at the end of a Stage)
- End Project Report (at the end of the project)
- Lessons Learned Report (at the end of the project)
- Exception Report (advance warning that Tolerance will not be met)
- Follow-on Action Recommendations (at the very end of the   project).

h) The End Project Report reviews benefits achieved *so far* at the end of Closing a Project (CP) process. The full set of benefits cannot be reviewed until some time after the project has ended.

3.5. Quality in a Project Environment

What's it all about?

P2 Quality is a bit like a jelly to a lot of people – it's difficult to get a firm grip on it. In fact, Quality is a collection of different things which, taken together across the Quality Path timeline, allow the project to:

- ❑ set and then meet expectations for following company policy on roles, tools, procedures, ISO 9000 etc
- ❑ set and then meet expectations for successful operation of the final project outcome, e.g. in terms of ownership, ease of use, reliability, factory yield and similar key characteristics
- ❑ negotiate between Users and Suppliers to agree functionality, size, shape etc of individual Products (deliverables), so that the Suppliers deliver what the users are expecting
- ❑ identify who will approve Products, how, and against what criteria.

An important aspect of Quality is that projects should actively *state* requirements, rather than guess or imply them.

Why Bother?

Agreeing the quality expectations of the Project Executive and Senior User(s) means that the Senior Supplier(s) can create Products that meet those expectations – quality will then have been achieved and it will be easier to get final acceptance at the end of the project. Also, Users may expect a level of Quality that cannot be achieved by Suppliers. The earlier this is discovered the better for everyone, since there is more time to negotiate expectations.

Understanding aspects of Quality such as reliability, ease of use, maintenance costs, factory yield and lifetime cost are an important pre-requisite to planning and delivering the right thing.

The Four Key Elements of Quality Management

There are four key areas that make up quality management:

- ❑ Quality System (QMS)
  This would include procedures, responsibilities, processes and tools. All projects need to follow appropriate standards that align the needs of the project with corporate norms and the need to interface with any separate user and supplier organisations.
- ❑ Quality Assurance
  This function sets up, runs and monitors the use of the quality systems within the host organisation, and should ideally be independent of all projects. If no independent group is available, Project Assurance would fulfil these duties within each individual project.

- ❑ Quality Planning

    This defines the requirements, objectives and activities for applying a QMS to the project. The Project Quality Plan within the PID is a key document that states how corporate norms will be applied to the whole project. Following on from this, specific requirements for a stage would be captured within a Stage Quality Plan, and quality criteria for individual Products stated within Product Descriptions.
- ❑ Quality Control

    This covers verification that completed Products meet their stated quality criteria; a PRINCE2 Quality Review is one of many ways to do this.

Key Facts

There is a **Quality Path** in PRINCE2 that follows the timeline of different aspects of quality from the customer's early quality expectations, through to delivery of completed Products that meet defined quality criteria.

There are many different aspects of Quality that come into play at different times in the Quality Path and project timeline; many have long names that are difficult to remember, so here's a checklist.

Aspects of Quality that are external to the project:
- ❑ **ISO**

    The International Standards Organisation (ISO) defines a range of quality standards, e.g. ISO 9001, that the project must meet. Adoption of PRINCE2 may help meet ISO standards.
- ❑ **Quality Policy**

    The host organisation should define the quality policy that a project needs to follow. For instance, a company that builds nuclear waste reprocessing equipment would have a more rigorous quality policy than a company that builds cheap houses.
- ❑ **Quality Management System (QMS)**

    A QMS is the set of day to day standards used by an organisation. A project should harmonise its' use of user and supplier QMS, so that the project is in line with corporate expectations and policy on quality.
- ❑ **Quality Assurance**

    There may be independent Quality Assurance people who have responsibility for ensuring that corporate standards are appropriate and actively used across all projects. Such responsibilities should be defined in the Project Quality Plan.
- ❑ **Project Mandate**

    Quality expectations and quality policy guidance might (or might not) be handed down to the project from higher level management as part of the Project Mandate.

Aspects of Quality during project start up and detailed definition:
- ❑ **Customer's Quality Expectations**

    These should be captured very early in the project as part of Preparing a Project Brief (SU4). They are a key input into planning Products and the activities to produce them.
- ❑ **Customer's Acceptance Criteria**

    The customer's measurable final acceptance criteria for the project as a whole, e.g. for reliability and ease of use. These are captured initially as part of Preparing a Project Brief (SU4) and then further developed during the Initiating a Project (IP) process. Confirmation that these criteria have been met is sought at the end of the project in CP1 Decommissioning a Project.

- ❑ **Project Approach**

  Quality expectations may influence decisions on whether the project will develop a solution in-house, outsource the development, make, buy or modify an existing solution. The Project Approach document describes and justifies such decisions.

- ❑ **Project Quality Plan**

  This defines how quality will be achieved in terms of roles, responsibilities, policies, procedures, templates, tools, Configuration Management etc, and should reference the corporate and supplier QMS where relevant. The Project Quality Plan is part of the Project Initiation Document (PID) created in Initiating a Project (IP) process.

- ❑ **Stage Quality Plans**

  These provide specific details of how quality will be achieved in a Stage. (The skills and methods required may vary from Stage to Stage. E.G. the way to check the quality of an art gallery building is different from the way to check the works of art within it.)

- ❑ **Project Assurance**

  This is an aspect of each Project Board member's duties and is frequently delegated to someone who can independently check that what the Project Manager is organising is appropriate. Project Assurance has a specific role to ensure that external (third party) Products are being defined and quality checked in an appropriately robust way.

Aspects of Quality during the 'doing' parts of a project:

- ❑ **Product Descriptions and Quality Criteria**

  As part of planning the project, every Product (deliverable) should have a Product Description defining the quality criteria for the finished Product, how those criteria will be assessed, and who will do the assessment. This is a quick win because (a) suppliers find out what they have to deliver and which users they need to communicate with, and (b) users get a chance to define what they want.

- ❑ **Work Packages**

  A Work Package is the mechanism for teams/suppliers to agree which Products they will create for the Project Manager, and to negotiate how they will work together in terms of reporting, escalation, key dates and costs. A Work Package references relevant Product Descriptions, and defines what quality policies, procedures, tools and other interfaces the team/supplier must use. A Work Package is therefore a key control of the quality of team/supplier work.

- ❑ **Quality Log**

  The Quality Log is created during IP. It has fields to record expected and actual dates for quality checking activities, and their outcome. Teams are responsible for proving that each Product meets the quality criteria previously defined in the Product Description for the Product, and will normally update the Quality Log with details of quality review activity.

- ❑ **Quality Control**

  Quality Control is the work of proving that Products meet their previously stated quality criteria. This may be done by testing samples of output (e.g. on a production line), or by using the Quality Review Technique.

- ❑ **Quality Review Technique**

  This is a way to prove that documentation Products meet the criteria set in their Product Descriptions, without the need for lengthy review meetings. However, the technique works for non-documentary Products too.

Other related key principles are:

- **End Stage Assessments and Approval of Products**

    During an End Stage Assessment (DP3), the Project Board formally confirms that the Products produced in the Stage just ending meet User and Supplier expectations; these Products are then known as 'Approved Products' and cannot be changed in the future without clearance from the Project Board. Newly approved Products are frequently baselined into the Configuration Library at this time.

- **Project Issues**

    Quality control may discover a problem with the Product being tested, or with a related Product. This situation is handled as an Issue. Off-Specification Products and Change Requests are aspects of quality that are also handled as Issues.

- **Off-Specification Products and Concessions**

    An 'Off-Specification Product' is one which does not meet it's quality criteria as defined in the previously agreed Product Description. If the Project Board decide to accept the Off-Specification Product, (e.g. because they will fix it later or it does not matter), this is called a Concession. Only the Project Board may grant a Concession.

- **Changes to Products**

    If a Change is made to a Product, its' Product Description must also be changed.

- **Post Project Review**

    The Post Project Review should review quality expectations against operational performance after a period of use.

Phrases to Remember

a) Quality is conformance to expectations.

b) Quality problems are handled as Project Issues.

c) Configuration Management plans are in the Project Quality Plan.

d) Quality requirements should be stated and not implied.

e) Subjective quality criteria such as 'must smell of apples' are OK, as long as you know who's making the judgement.

f) Only the Project Board may change an *Approved* Product.

3.6. Plans

What's it all about?

Plans contain definitions of deliverables, activities, dates, costs, resource requirements, often in Gantt chart format, plus accompanying text to justify and explain why things are the way they are. Larger projects may require separate Stage Plans as well as a Project Plan. All plans have the same format. Team plans are optional, although teams should be encouraged to use PRINCE2 where relevant.

An Exception Plan is a draft replacement Stage Plan presented to the Project Board to correct a previous Exception that was predicted to push the Stage or project outside a previously agreed Tolerance.

Why bother?

Plans are estimates of whether a target is achievable, how it will be reached, and what resources will be required. Without a Plan there is little chance of reaching a business target.

The Project Board reviews the Project Plan and Stage Plans prior to Stage commencement, and decides whether to commit the resources required for the next Stage as defined in the Stage Plan. The Project Manager then runs the Stage Plan on a day to day basis until the next End Stage Assessment.

Plans are the basis of day to day delegation and control. They should be as detailed as necessary to meet the needs of the plan owner, plus provide tracking information to report to others above and below the plan owner.

Key Facts

The Project Plan and Stage Plans might have been created before the project started, following previous research, feasibility studies or programme work, and be given to the project as part of the Project Mandate.

Initial expectations about the Plan (key dates, costs and key Products) are captured in the Project Brief created in SU4. This information is expanded during Initiating a Project (IP) process into an overview of the whole project. The project Plan is a major part of the Project Initiation Document (PID) created during Initiating a Project (IP) process. Stage Plans are created towards the end of a Stage as described in the Managing Stage Boundaries (SB) process.

Ongoing progress information is added to the Plans as part of Controlling a Stage (CS) process. Towards the end of each Stage, the next Stage Plan is created in the Managing Stage Boundaries (SB) process, and then presented to the Project Board at the End Stage Assessment. If the Project Board approves the Plan, the Project Manager is given the authority to execute the Plan on a day to day basis, within a Tolerance agreed with the Project Board. Higher risk Plans should have less Tolerance.

Phrases to Remember

a) A Project Plan is the backbone of every project.

b) All P2 Plans have the same format.

c) Plans are more than just a Gantt chart.

d) Team plans are optional.

e) The Project Plan is mandatory, separate Stage Plans are optional. In a small project the plans for Stages will be held within the Project Plan.

f) During IP, projects must decide what number and type of Plans to have.

g) Tiny projects may have just a Product Checklist rather than an activity plan or Gantt chart.

3.7. Risk Management

What's it all about?

Risk management is an attitude of mind. Poor risk management often leads to large numbers of unexpected problems, delivery out of Tolerance or disappointed users. Eliminating all risk is usually neither desirable nor possible; Project Boards must decide what is the right level of risk to take in a particular project.

The P2 method defines:

- ❑ **Risk Analysis**
  Identification and evaluation of risks and their countermeasures. Risk analysis produces data such as probability, impact, proximity, owner, countermeasures that are captured in the Risk Log.

- ❑ **Risk Management**
  Day to day actioning of countermeasures throughout the project.

Why Bother?

Risks are future threats that you know about now, however they may or may not happen. If they did happen they would prevent the Plans from coming true, causing problems in the project and loss of benefits.

If risks actually happen they become Project Issues. If there are too many Project Issues in a project there is probably not much risk management going on.

Sometimes it is necessary to increase the level of risk in a project, e.g. shorten the plan so the project finishes earlier, expecting that some aspect of the project will not go to Plan.

People who are good at risk management cope with uncertainty better and their Plans come true more often.

Key Facts

Initial views of key risks may (or may not) be identified in the Project Mandate.

Key risks are described within the Project Brief created in Starting Up a Project (SU) process, so that the Project Board can get a high level early view of the risks as well as the benefits of the project.

The Risk Log is created during SU4. (Most other logs are created in IP).

During the Initiating a Project (IP) process, the risks and risk management actions are defined in detail. The Project Board will be asked to approve and commit to these risk management actions at the end of IP when they approve the PID (DP2).

Risks should always be analysed as part of doing Starting up a Project (SU) process, Planning (PL) process and Authorising a Work Package (CS1).

Plans should be reviewed and modified after the risks have been analysed. It may be necessary to:

- ❑ change the duration of some activities
  e.g. to allow more time for creation of a Product that is not expected to be right first time
- ❑ add new activities
  e.g. send an expert to work with a supplier to improve quality of their output
- ❑ change the resourcing of activities
  e.g. to use more experienced staff on higher risk tasks
- ❑ re-plan the deliverables and activities
  e.g. do things in a different way if the original plan is too risky
- ❑ make a contingency plan
  e.g. an alternative set of actions that will be invoked if the risk happens.

Everyone should concentrate on lowering the probability of risks so that fewer of them become Project Issues. (It is better for a boat to stay afloat than to use the wonderful lifeboats.)

The Project Board should review the key risks at End Stage Assessments, to ensure that the right level of risk is being taken, and that the level of risk is balanced with the benefits in the Business Case.

Acceptance of a risk is dangerous, however is a valid strategy if:

a) there is nothing you can do about the risk
b) you honestly believe the risk will never happen
c) if it did happen it would not hurt much.

Denial of a risk is not valid strategy, and not a good career move either.

The following must happen for every risk:

- ❑ **Risk Analysis**
  This consists of recognising what risks exist, analysing their importance and deciding what you *intend* to do about them. The results of Risk Analysis are stored in the Risk Log.

Key Risk Log contents are:

description – a description of the risk
probability – how likely it is to occur
potential impact – what would happen if it did occur
proximity – how far away in time the impact would be
owner – the best person to keep an eye on the risk
potential countermeasures – options to reduce probability and/or impact
actual countermeasures – the selected countermeasure(s) to be actioned on the basis of cost and impact of mitigation being proportionate to the impact if the risk were to happen.

❑ **Risk Management**
This consists of actual day to day actions that reduce the probability and/or potential impact of the risk.

Plan – Change the activities to add the chosen countermeasures.
Resource – Allocate resources (time, cost, people, equipment, space etc) for the chosen countermeasures.
Monitor – Check that the countermeasures are working.
Report – To keep higher authorities informed and to seek their support.

Phrases to Remember
a) Valid strategies for risk countermeasures are 'the four Ts' – Tolerate, Treat, Terminate and Transfer. Cost effective actions should be identified that are 'P R A C T' - seeking to either/or Prevent, Reduce, Accept, Contingency, Transfer the probability and/or impact of a risk.
b) Denial of a risk is NOT a valid option.
c) Risks are defined as uncertainty of outcome.
d) Project Boards need to decide what is the right level of risk for a project. Sometimes they should *increase* the level of risk in a project, e.g. shortening a project to hit a market window.
e) Risks are uncertainties about the future. Project Issues are problems (and/or Change Requests) that have already happened or are certain to happen in the future.
f) As minimum, the Risk Log should be updated towards the end of a Stage, within the Managing Stage Boundaries (SB) process.
g) It is better to focus on reducing the probability of risks occurring rather than being very good at handling Issues.

3.8. Change Control

What's it all about?

Handling of requests for changes to any previously approved aspect of a project, e.g. a request to add functionality to a Product.

The method describes change in a fragmented way spread across several chapters:

Can you fit a roof-rack?

- ❑ **Change Control Component chapter**
  Describes what change is, the difference between good and bad changes, and why change should be managed
- ❑ **Change Control Technique chapter**
  Describes how to process prioritised Change Requests in the same way as Project Issues
- ❑ **Parts of Controlling a Stage Process chapter**
  Describes day to day processing of Project Issues and Change Requests by the Project Manager.

Changes can be requested by anyone, and may come from inside the project or the outside world. Users often want changes to previously agreed functionality, and business leaders often make changes that affect what the project is being asked to do. If change is not managed it can be very damaging to a project.

Why Bother?

Although P2 encourages creation of credible plans and then their controlled execution, changes to those plans are inevitable. Change must be managed to ensure that beneficial changes are adopted and undesirable changes rejected. Too much change can be a major threat to successful completion of a Plan.

The Project Board approves Plans at End Stage Assessments and then gives the Project Manager authority to run that Plan within a Tolerance. The Project Manager makes decisions about change as long as they still believe they will finish the Stage and Project within Tolerance. The Project Board must decide on any major changes that would push the Plan out of Tolerance if they were implemented.

Just because a request for change has been made it does not mean that the Project Manager has to implement it. A change request can be rejected if it is not beneficial, or if this is the wrong time to do it. Poor change control can undermine the Business Case and cause major commercial problems, especially to Suppliers on fixed price contracts.

Key Facts

The Project Mandate may give early warning of anticipated changes.

All changes are handled as Project Issues. Project Issues must be captured in the Issue Log (CS3 Capturing Project Issues) and have their impact assessed (CS4 Examining Project Issues) by appropriate people from the User, Supplier and Business community. Project Assurance can advise on who should be involved, and can assess the impact of the Change Request on the Business Case, Plans and risks.

Change Request handling should be prioritised – the method suggests 5 levels of priority in the Change Control Technique chapter.

The Project Manager can take decisions on changes provided that the changes do not trigger a forecast that the Stage or project will finish out of Tolerance.

The Project Board may define a Change Authority role with a Change Budget to make decisions about change on their behalf.

Confusingly, the Change Control Component chapter of the method also defines:

- ❏ **Off-Specification Products**
  These are Products that do not meet the quality criteria defined in their Product Description (which was written when the Stage was planned).
- ❏ **Concessions**
  An agreement by the Project Board to accept an Off-Specification product because either it is not a significant problem, or they will fix it later (perhaps in another project).

Phrases to Remember
a) Change is inevitable.
b) Change is handled as a Project Issue.
c) A good change is one where the benefit exceeds the impact of making the change.
d) Only the Project Board may authorise a change to an *approved* Product (a deliverable completed in a previous Stage.)
e) A beneficial change request may trigger an Exception situation.
f) Change Control and Configuration Management are very closely linked.

3.9. Configuration Management

What's it all about?

Configuration Management is all about procedures and systems to control multiple versions of Products. It includes:

- records of who has got what, where and why
- records of any changes made
- a library and librarian role
- decisions about what tools and procedures to use to run the library
- decisions about what to put in the library and how to number the versions
- multiple baselined versions of Products
- occasional reports and audits to verify that records match reality.

This sounds like bureaucracy to many people, however like most of PRINCE2 it is highly scaleable and *needs* to be tailored to the right level of detail and formality. The configuration management requirements of a small, short project are quite different from those of a project to build a nuclear waste reprocessing plant. The method describes general principles; project managers must decide *to what extent, and how* these principles should be applied.

Why Bother?

Changes to Plans and Products are inevitable, so multiple versions will be created. Failure to keep appropriate records of what versions exist, what was changed and why, leads to chaos.

Auditors require records of how changes and versions are controlled, especially in public sector organisations and public companies.

You may need to go back to a previous version of something.

You may need to repair or enhance an old version of a Product that is in live usage somewhere, e.g. to repair a defect that has been reported by users.

Key Facts

Configuration library services are often provided by the host organisation, in which case a project just needs to use the service. This is because many of the Products produced by projects have a life before and after the project.

Configuration Plans and decisions about tools, procedures and responsibilities are made during the Initiating a Project (IP) process and documented within the Project Quality Plan that is part of the Project Initiation Document (PID).

Configuration Management consists of 5 parts.

Product Submission
When a new version of a Product is ready, a new Baseline version (a new frozen snapshot in time) is submitted to the configuration library.

Issuing Copies
The library giving out read only copies, e.g. giving a read only copy of a Requirement Specification to a testing team.

Product Issue
The library handing out a controlled copy for modification, e.g. giving an editable copy of a Requirement Specification back to the author for update.

Status Accounting
The library maintaining records and producing reports about who has what, and any changes made to Products.

Verification
The library auditing its' records to ensure that the records match reality, e.g. an end of Stage audit to ensure that only authorised copies of key Products exist.

Phrases to Remember
a) Configuration Management and Change Control work together very closely.
b) The assets of a project are the Products it produces.
c) Configuration Management can be thought of as asset control or version control.
d) Configuration Management records can tell you the state of any Product at any time.
e) The Configuration Librarian maintains the Issue Log.
f) The Project Manager is responsible for Configuration Management.

Chapter 4.   The 8 PRINCE2 Processes

4.1.   One Minute Overview

The 8 Processes are like the instructions for making an apple pie from a pile of ingredients. The ingredients of a project are the 8 PRINCE2 Components, and the way to use the ingredients is to follow the 45 separate steps described in the 8 PRINCE2 Processes.

The 8 Processes are:

- **Directing a Project (DP) process**
  Contains 5 sub-processes describing how the Project Board should steer the project.
- **Starting up a Project (SU) process**
  Contains 6 sub-processes describing pre-project preparation - how to qualify initial ideas before formally commencing the project.
- **Initiating a Project (IP) process**
  Contains 6 sub-processes describing detailed definition before starting hands on development work.
- **Controlling a Stage (CS) process**
  Contains 9 sub-processes describing the day to day work of the Project Manager when executing a Plan.
- **Managing Product Delivery (MP) process**
  Contains 3 sub-processes describing the day to day work of the Team Manager(s) who manage the creation of Products (deliverables) required by the Project Manager.
- **Managing Stage Boundaries (SB) process**
  Contains 6 sub-processes describing the work of the Project Manager to prepare for an End Stage Assessment or Exception Assessment by the Project Board.
- **Planning (PL) process**
  Contains 7 sub-processes describing how to define deliverables and create a credible activity Plan. This process can be used at any time throughout the project.
- **Closing a Project (CP) process**
  Contains 3 sub-processes describing formal closure, handover and review of the project.

Phrases to Remember

a) Before using a process you should decide *how extensively* and how formally the process should be applied.

b) All processes should be tailored to suit local requirements, and need not be formal and paper based.

c) The Project Manager and Project Board must decide *to what extent* each process applies to each project.

4.2. Directing a Project (DP) Process

Purpose

This process describes the decision making and governance work of the Project Board throughout the whole project life cycle.

The Directing a Project (DP) process describes:

- ❑ 3 formal decision making points that occur at a specific time in the project lifecycle (DP1, DP2, DP5)
- ❑ a general purpose reusable decision making point (DP3) either a) at the end of any 'doing' Stage, or b) when reviewing an Exception Plan
- ❑ general purpose communication and governance at any point between Stage boundaries (DP4).

Note: The structure and roles within a Project Board are NOT defined in DP, they are defined in the Organisation component chapter of the method.

Why Bother?

The Project Board provides the interface between the project and programmes, corporate bodies or the outside world. The purpose of the Project Board is to:

- ❑ run projects to achieve beneficial changes
  e.g. to create new company products and services
- ❑ provide governance
  e.g. make decisions about Plans, commit resources, and give authority to spend
- ❑ represent more senior management in running of the project
  e.g. report on project progress to more senior management and react to any new instructions from more senior management
- ❑ support and steer the Project Manager
  e.g. providing advice, making decisions and solving problems at management level
- ❑ stop projects that are no longer desirable
  e.g. if the market conditions have changed and the project is no longer needed.

Key Facts

In general terms the Project Board always does the same thing:

- ❑ formally reviews the project at an End Stage Assessment
  This is often a meeting, however any appropriate meeting of minds will do nicely. Telephone calls and video conferences can save a lot of time.

- ❑ confirms whether the reasons for running a project are still valid
- ❑ aligns the project with corporate or programme guidance
- ❑ reviews progress
- ❑ reviews plans for the future
- ❑ reviews key risks and Project Issues
- ❑ decides whether to proceed, redirect or stop the project.

If they decide to proceed, the Project Board commit resources to the Plan and give the Project Manager authority to spend those resources within a decision making Tolerance.

A Project Board should NOT decide to proceed unless:

- ❑ the Project Board members have all the necessary resources to execute the next Stage as described in the Plan presented to them by the Project Manager. (If they don't, the Stage length should be shortened until they do.)
- ❑ the Plan is acceptable to more senior management
  e.g. it fits with corporate or programme strategy
- ❑ the Plan has the right level of risk within it
  e.g. looks realistic and credible without being too slow
- ❑ the Senior User(s), Senior Supplier(s) and Project Executive fully support it
- ❑ the three Project Assurance roles agree the Plan and Business Case are credible.

There are 5 sub-processes within Directing a Project (DP) process.

DP1 Authorising Initiation
DP actually starts during SU, however the first formal act of the Project Board is at the end of SU, to review early high level expectations, then decide whether to proceed into detailed definition and planning as described in the Initiating a Project (IP) process.

DP2 Authorising a Project
Review detailed definition of the project before commencing the first 'doing' Stage, based on information developed in the Project Initiation Document (PID).

DP3 Authorising a Stage or Exception Plan
This is an End Stage Assessment at the end of any 'doing' Stage, to decide whether to proceed further with the project. DP3 is also used during a Stage to review an Exception Plan prepared by the Project Manager if the Stage or project is forecast to exceed Tolerance.

DP5 Confirming Project Closure
Final confirmation that the project really has finished, that all the deliverables meet previously agreed quality expectations, and that the customer is happy. DP5 also includes review of the whole project against original expectations at the end of IP, and organisation of a Post Project Review to take place in the future.

DP4 Giving Ad-hoc Direction
Project Board communication, reporting, advice and decision making at any other time in the project.

Management by Exception

The Project Board gives authority to the Project Manager to run the Plan for the next Stage within a Tolerance (of time, cost, quality, scope, benefit or risk). The Project Manager then takes day to day responsibility for executing the Plan, and must escalate to the Project Board *as soon as* they start to forecast that completion of the Stage or project within Tolerance is no longer possible.

Project Board Information Sources

The Project Board members have a number of different information sources from which they can make judgements about the project.

❑ **End Stage Report**

A summary from the Project Manager (written in SB5 Reporting Stage End). This contains a summary of past, present and future Plans, major risks and Project Issues, key decisions to be made, options, recommendations and any major learning points.

❑ **New corporate or programme guidance**

New information from higher up the business or the outside world.

❑ **Reasons for the project**

The Business Case, plus other management information and judgement will state why the project is being run.

❑ **Progress**

Progress is summarised within Highlight Reports and the End Stage Report, based on details stored within the Project and current Stage Plan.

❑ **Expectations for the future**

A summary of future Plans is provided within the End Stage Report, based on details stored within the Project and next Stage Plan.

❑ **Key risks**

The Risk Log contains information about what risks exist, their probability, potential impact and countermeasures.

❑ **Key Project Issues and Change Requests**

The Issue Log contains information about Project Issues that require management intervention, plus any Change Requests.

❑ **Other management information**

Project Board members will have access to management information that is not specifically handled by P2. E.G. general information will be circulating amongst business management but will not be written into one or other P2 data sets.

Most of these data sources are created or updated by the Project Manager in Managing Stage Boundaries (SB) process towards the end of the current Stage, in preparation for an End Stage Assessment.

4.3. Starting Up a Project (SU) Process

Purpose

This process is aimed at getting a quick, early view of the general size and shape of the project to:

- ❑ confirm that the project looks like a sensible idea before investing in detailed planning
- ❑ identify the key stakeholders and teams, and to seek their views and involvement
- ❑ capture expectations for quality and operational Acceptance Criteria
- ❑ gather together existing information about the project.

If extensive preparation work has already been done, and a Project Board is already in place, the SU process can be fast tracked.

Why Bother?

The project may have seemed like a good idea in the bar on a Friday night, but is it still a good idea in the harsh light of a Monday morning?

SU lays the foundations for everything that comes later in a project. It captures early views on:

- ❑ the expected benefits from running the project
- ❑ the approach that the project will take
  e.g. whether to make, buy, modify or outsource a solution
- ❑ plans and key deliverables
- ❑ quality expectations and key acceptance criteria
- ❑ obvious risks
- ❑ who should be involved in managing the project
- ❑ expected project duration and cost
- ❑ whether the project is viable and worthwhile.

These early views are captured in the Project Brief and Project Approach documents that are presented to the Project Board at the DP1 Authorising Initiation assessment. If the Project Board decide to invest further in the project, the Initiating a Project (IP) process is used to expand early views from SU into much greater detail.

Key Facts

Receipt of a Project Mandate is the trigger to start doing the SU process.

The Project Mandate can come from anywhere and take any form – it does not have to be written down. It might be a verbal instruction, a fully developed set of Plans, or a Work Package from a DIFFERENT project.

There are 6 sub-processes within Starting up a Project (SU) process.

SU1 Appointing a Project Board Executive and Project Manager
The Project Executive and Project Manager are appointed. Frequently the Project Executive will have provided the Project Mandate.

SU2 Designing a Project Management Team
Deciding how the 9 PRINCE2 roles should implemented. E.G. who should be asked to fill each role, and what roles should be split, shared or combined.

SU3 Appointing a Project Management Team
This is negotiation with people to agree their roles, time commitment and duties within the project. This turns the draft job descriptions (from SU2) into agreed job descriptions.

SU4 Preparing a Project Brief
Write the Project Brief and create the Risk Log, Daily Log and Outline Business Case.

The Project Brief is a high level early view of the project, including scope, objectives, quality expectations (e.g. reliability and ease of use), outline Business Case, key deliverables (Products), key risks, guesstimates of timescales and costs, plus customers' quality expectations and final operational acceptance criteria such as ease of use and reliability.

The Risk Log is used throughout the project to record the results of Risk Analysis activity and proposed countermeasures.

SU5 Defining Project Approach
Write the Project Approach document that records decisions on whether to do the project in-house or outsourced, plus make, buy, modify and similar decisions. The Senior Supplier will have significant input into deciding the best approach because of the feasibility/time/cost/risk/quality balance they are being asked to commit to.

SU6 Planning an Initiation Stage
Plan the next Stage (which will always be the mandatory Initiation Stage). During the Initiation Stage the project must build up a lot of detail about how it will operate (Plans, Controls etc). It is sensible for the Project Board to approve the investment first, since creating this detail could be a major time and cost commitment.

Phrases to Remember
a) SU is *pre-project preparation*.
b) The first formal act of the Project Board (DP1 Authorising Initiation) is at the end of SU, however the DP process starts during SU.
c) Different Project Approaches will lead to radically different Plans and risks.
d) The Risk Log and Daily Log are created in SU. (There are 5 logs defined in PRINCE2 – the Issue Log, Quality Log and Lessons Learned Log are all created in IP).
e) An important part of SU4 is capturing the customer's quality expectations and overall acceptance criteria – these will greatly influence the project Plan and quality criteria of individual Products (deliverables).

4.4. Initiating a Project (IP) Process

Purpose

The purpose of the Initiating a Project (IP) process is to define in detail as much of the project as is visible at the time, so that the Project Board can decide whether or not to commence the hands-on development work of the project.

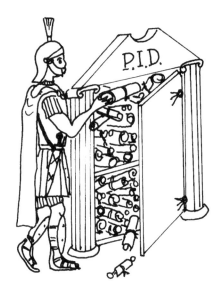

The Starting Up a Project (SU) process produced an early outline view of the project documented in the Project Brief and Project Approach documents. This early view is expanded in IP to create as much fully qualified detail as possible. The longer the project the more sketchy the distant future will be.

The Initiating a Project (IP) process explains how to expand the key outputs from SU (Project Brief, Project Approach and Risk Log) into the Project Initiation Document (PID).

Why Bother?

The key output of IP is the Project Initiation Document (PID). This is often more like a filing cabinet than a document, consisting of many different sets of information structured into major sections. The PID contains all of the major information sets used throughout the rest of the project:

- ❏ Business Case – a justification of why the project is beneficial
- ❏ Plans – Product definitions, activities, dates, costs, resources
- ❏ Controls – governance arrangements at all levels
- ❏ Quality – policies, tools, methods, roles, use of corporate standards
- ❏ Organisation – roles and decision making authority
- ❏ Risk Log – contains the results of a Risk Analysis

IP is valuable because it gets user, supplier and business interests working together to put this level of understanding in place. Teams find out what they have to deliver and have an opportunity to negotiate any unreasonable user requirements. Business interests find out whether a business target is achievable, and at what cost and effort.

Key Facts

The Initiating a Project (IP) process consists of 6 sub-processes, most of which are just pointers to different parts of the method. IP integrates together all of the PRINCE2 components into a coherent set of information that defines what the project will do, and how it intends to go about it.

There are 6 sub-processes in the Initiating a Project (IP) process.

IP1 Planning Quality

This is a trigger to decide *how* the quality regime for the project will work, in terms of policies, procedures, tools, methods, configuration management and the relationship to corporate standards of the host organisation and any external suppliers. Much of this will be pre-defined for a project as part of normal working practices, however it should always be reviewed to make sure it is appropriate for the scale and formality of the project.

Key outputs are:

Project Quality Plan
Contains definitions of all aspects of Quality for the whole project, including Configuration Management arrangements and how quality will be achieved.

Quality Log
A log, principally for audit purposes, that will hold details of all quality checking activity in the project. For example, it will include expected and actual dates of Quality Reviews, and their outcome.

IP2 Planning a Project

This is a trigger to use the Planning (PL) process which in turn invokes the Product Based Planning (PBP) technique to produce the Project Plan. Decisions will have to be made on the number and length of Stages, whether Stage Plans are required in addition to the Project Plan, and whether teams will have separate Team Plans.

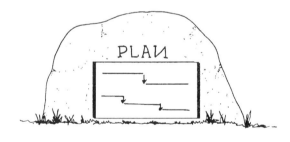

The key outputs are:
Project Plan
Mandatory in P2. In a large project this will usually be a summary plan, with details defined within Stage Plans. Tiny projects may only need a Product Checklist rather than detailed activity definitions.

Change Authority and Change Budget
The Project Board may delegate decisions on change to a Change Authority person or group. It's also sensible to allocate a budget in terms of time/cost/risk/quality for individual changes and the total set of changes accepted in a Stage.

IP3 Refining the Business Case and Risks
The Business Case is written in IP (if it has not already been written outside the project), and a full risk analysis undertaken. (Throughout the rest of the project, whenever the Project Plan is changed the Business Case needs to be updated and the Risk Analysis revised.)

Key outputs are:

Business Case
The Business Case is expanded/written based on the facts provided by the Plans and any further market projection work that has been done.

Risk Log updates
The Risk Analysis should concentrate on key threats to the Business Case coming true.

Project Plan updates
Plans should be modified to mitigate any unacceptable risks, or to raise the level of risk if the Plan is too risk averse.

IP4 Setting up Project Controls
This is a trigger to decide which of the 26 Controls to use, and how they will be implemented. Controls are needed throughout the project in the same way that the controls of a car are needed throughout a journey. Different controls are needed to do different things at different times.

Key outputs are:

Project Controls
Definitions of which Controls will be used, and how. Key decisions will relate to content and frequency of Highlight Reports and Checkpoint Reports.

Communications Plan
An agreement stating what information will be sent, to whom, when, why, in what format, and how feedback systems will work.

IP5 Setting up Project Files
This is a trigger to decide what filing and archiving systems are needed. It is sensible to have a structured filing system for both electronic and physical Products, documents etc. Appendix E of the PRINCE2 manual suggests a directory structure.

The Issue Log and Lessons Learned Log should be created in IP5.

IP6 Assembling a Project Initiation Document

A Project Initiation Document (PID) is a collection of information stating what the project will do, how it will do it, and what policies, procedures, roles etc it will use. In a large project the PID will be more like a filing cabinet than a single document – an extensive collection of interrelated data about the project and how it will be run. The various parts of the PID should be consistent with each other.

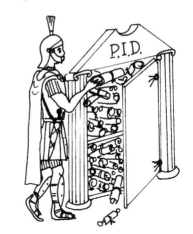

A PID is assembled in IP6 by bringing together outputs from IP1 to IP5, in particular the Plans, Business Case, Controls, Risks and Quality arrangements.

IP1 to IP5 will normally need to be repeated more than once until the user, supplier and business interests are content that the Plans, Business Case and risks are reasonable and acceptable. Once this consensus has been achieved the Project Initiation Document (PID) should be assembled in IP6 from its' many different parts created earlier in IP. IP6 also triggers creation of the Next Stage Plan by invoking the Managing Stage Boundaries process (SB1 Planning a Stage).

The PID and Next Stage Plan are presented to the Project Board at their End Stage Assessment at the end of IP (DP2 Authorising a Project). If they approve the PID, it becomes the contract between Project Manager and Project Board for what the project must deliver.

Phrases to Remember
a) The Project Quality Plan describes *how* quality will be achieved across the project.
b) Stage Quality plans give details of the quality control in individual Stages.
c) The Configuration Management Plan is a section of the Project Quality Plan which is a section of the Project Initiation Document (PID).
d) Product Description and the Issue Log are filed in the Quality area of the filing system.
e) The Risk Log is filed as part of the project area of the management file.
f) Initiating a Project (IP) process is considered mandatory, even for very small projects.
g) The volatile parts of the PID (Project Plan, Risk Log, Business Case) will get updated towards the end of each Stage. This is triggered by the Managing Stage Boundaries (SB) process.
h) The End Project Report produced in Closing a Project (CP) process reviews actual project events against expectations within the original PID assembled in IP6.

4.5.   Controlling a Stage (CS) Process

Purpose

The Controlling a Stage (CS) process is the day to day work of the Project Manager from after the Project Board approve the Project Initiation Document (PID) in DP2 Authorising a Project, until commencement of the Closing a Project (CP) process.

There are 9 sub-processes within Controlling a Stage process, however they are structured into 5 main topic areas:

- ❑ Reporting to the Project Board
    - CS6 Reporting Highlights
- ❑ Handling teams or suppliers
    - CS1 Authorising a Work Package
    - CS2 Assessing Progress
    - CS9 Receiving a Complete Work Package
- ❑ Capturing and assessing problems and Change Requests
    - CS3 Capturing Project Issues
    - CS4 Examining Project Issues
- ❑ Deciding what needs to happen next
    - CS5 Reviewing Stage Status
- ❑ Reacting when the Plan needs to change
    - CS7 Taking Corrective Action
    - CS8 Escalating Project Issues

Why bother?

Once the Project Board have approved a Project Plan and/or a Stage Plan and set a Tolerance, it is the Project Managers' responsibility to organise day to day events so that the activities within the Plan happen and the Products (deliverables) required are created.

The Project Manager has authority to execute a Plan and spend the resources granted to them by the Project Board. A Project Manager can make decisions and adjust the Plan if necessary, *as long as they still believe the Stage and project can be completed within the previously agreed Tolerance.* However, *as soon as* the Project Manager believes that Tolerance cannot be met, they have lost their authority to proceed and must escalate the situation to the Project Board. This is called Management by Exception. (The steps to follow to do the escalation are called Exception Handling).

Key Facts

The Controlling a Stage (CS) process invokes the Managing Product Delivery (MP) process whenever the Project Manager is dealing with teams. It is sensible to consider CS1, CS2 and CS9 in parallel with MP1, MP2 and MP3.

CS1 Authorising a Work Package/MP1 Accepting a Work Package

A Work Package is a negotiated agreement on which Products the Team Manager will create and how this team will work with the Project Manager. The formality and terms of a Work Package will vary according to the level of trust in the team; it should be negotiated by the Team Manager (in MP1 Accepting a Work Package) and Project Manager working together.

A Work Package should define:

- ❏ frequency and content of reports
- ❏ key milestone dates and costs
- ❏ interfaces to other teams and communication lines
- ❏ procedures for escalation of problems, Change Requests and key risks
- ❏ an agreed Tolerance for delivery of the completed Work Package.

CS2 Assessing Progress/MP2 Executing a Work Package

MP2 Executing a Work Package is the work of the Team Manager in managing creation of Products. The team will generate Checkpoint Reports containing progress information at a frequency agreed in the Work Package. This Checkpoint Report and progress information is received by the Project Manager is CS2. Note that *reacting* to the progress information is defined in CS5, CS7 and CS8, not here is CS2.

The team should update the Quality Log to record the outcome of any quality checking activity.

CS9 Receiving a Completed Work Package/MP3 Delivering a Work Package

The team returns the completed Work Package and associated completed Products back to the Project Manager *after* the Products have been proved to meet the quality criteria stated in their Product Descriptions.

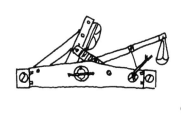

A team may use the Quality Review technique to prove that a Product is finished.

CS3 Capturing Project Issues

Project Issues may come from any source, may cover any topic, and may or may not be urgent. Procedures should be set up to handle them centrally in a consistent and timely manner. CS3 captures Project Issues and puts them into the Issue Log (created in IP) for tracking purposes.

The method is fragmented in its definition of Project Issues and how to handle them. It is more important to understand the value of issue handling than to understand why the manual is the way it is.

Project Issues are formally defined within the manual in:

- ❑ Change Control Component chapter
- ❑ Change Control Technique chapter.

There are 4 types of Project Issue:

- ❑ **Off-Specifications**
  Products that do not meet their previously agreed quality criteria.
- ❑ **Questions** (includes new facts)
  Non-trivial problems and queries that require management intervention to resolve and are worthy of formal impact assessment. E.G. any question, new information, external data, emails or other information that needs to be handled formerly by the project.
- ❑ **Statements of Concern**
  Any comment from stakeholders requiring formal investigation and response.
- ❑ **Requests for Change**
  E.G. a request to change the functionality of a Product.

  PRINCE2 suggests 5 levels of priority for Change Requests:
  1. Must have
  2. Important
  3. Nice to have
  4. Cosmetic of no importance
  5. Not a change

A Project Support service is often responsible for capturing and logging Project Issues centrally, on behalf of the Project Manager.

CS4 Examining Project Issues

The Project Manager should assess the priority of new Project Issues and ensure appropriate reaction times.

Appropriately skilled people from User, Supplier AND Business communities should assess the full lifetime impact of a Project Issue or Change Request. The impact of the Project Issue should be examined against existing Plans, Business Case and risks so that any decisions are based on facts rather than gut feel.

Project Assurance (from any or all of the three project interest areas) can advise on who should be consulted about a Project Issue, and are likely to have opinions on impact themselves.

The end point of CS4 is an understanding of the impact of a Project Issue; deciding what to do next lies within CS5.

CS5 Reviewing Stage Status

This is the P2 equivalent of the Project Managers brain, deciding whether the Stage is still on schedule to finish within the Tolerance previously agreed with the Project Board. There are many inputs, in particular Checkpoint Reports from teams and data from Issue, Risk and Quality Logs.

When reviewing Stage status there are only 3 possible conclusions the Project Manager can reach:

- It's all going very well
  No changes to the Stage Plan and Products are required.
- Minor changes are needed (CS7)
  Activities need to have minor corrective changes (via CS7), however we can still finish within the previously agreed Tolerance.
- It's all going horribly wrong
  Tolerance will be exceeded, therefore the situation must be escalated to the Project Board (via CS8).

CS6 Reporting Highlights

The Project Manager should send Highlight Reports to the Project Board on a regular time basis, at a timing, frequency and content agreed with the Project Board at the previous End Stage Assessment.

Key contents of Highlight Reports are:
- progress against Plan
- key risks and Project Issues
- update on quality status, time and cost
- any likely problem areas.

The Project Board receive the Highlight Report in DP4, and may provide advice, feedback and new management information to the Project Manager.

CS7 Taking Corrective Action

The Project Manager may need to adjust the activities to take corrective action because of real world events. This is perfectly acceptable as long as the Stage or project is still forecast to complete within Tolerance.

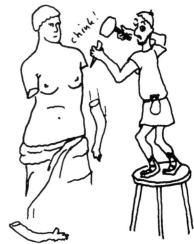

CS8 Escalating Project Issues

The Project Manager MUST escalate to the Project Board *as soon as* it is forecast that the Stage or Project Plan cannot be completed within the Tolerance previously agreed with the Project Board. Escalation is achieved through an Exception Report. (See Exception Handling for full explanation of the process steps for handling out of Tolerance situations.)

Phrases to Remember
a) A Work Package is the *only* mechanism in the method for handing out work to a team or supplier.
b) Some teams may be internal, others may be third party organisations.
c) A Work Package might be a Project Mandate to a supplier that uses PRINCE2 at team level.
d) Long technical/specialist team work should be divided into multiple Work Packages that start and finish within a Stage. This forces out interim deliverables and makes it much easier to assess progress.
e) Anyone may raise a Project Issue, and all Project Issues are handled in the same way.
f) Receipt of a Project Issue should be acknowledged back to the originator.
g) The Issue Log is maintained by the Configuration Librarian, who by default is the Project Manager.
h) Highlight Reports may provide early warning of a future out of Tolerance forecast.
i) The project is in Exception *as soon as* it is forecast that the current Stage Plan or Project Plan cannot be completed within the previously agreed Tolerance.
j) Since there may be several teams and many Work Packages, the CS process invokes the Managing Product Delivery (MP) process on a *frequent and iterative basis*.
k) The CS process does NOT invoke the Planning (PL) process, because planning the next Stage is triggered from within the Managing Stage Boundaries (SB) process, not from within CS.

4.6. Managing Product Delivery (MP) Process

Purpose
This process defines the work of the Team Manager(s) to manage the creation of Products. It is straightforward because most of team work is outside of the method. The Managing Product Delivery (MP) process covers negotiating Work Packages, executing them, escalating any forecast Exception situations then handing them back *after* they have been proved to be complete.

Why Bother?
The Managing Product Delivery (MP) process is the Team Manager's side of Work Packages. The Work Package mechanism is the only way to formally hand out work in a P2 project. Work Packages can be defined with any level of formality, irrespective of whether the team is internal or a third party.

Key Facts
The Managing Product Delivery (MP1, MP2, MP3) sub-processes link directly to the Controlling a Stage (CS1, CS2, CS9) sub-processes to provide a standard interface between the Project Manager and teams/suppliers. The emphasis is on defining Products (deliverables) to be produced, and how the team should work with the Project Manager on a day to day basis. Contracts and Service Level Agreements are not defined in the method, however Work Packages and Product Descriptions may overlap with or add value to them.

MP1 Accepting a Work Package/CS1 Authorising a Work Package
This describes negotiation of a Work Package by the Team Manager.
(See CS1 for fuller explanation).

MP2 Executing a Work Package/CS2 Assessing Progress
This sub-process covers management of all the team activities necessary to create the required Products and get them accepted. A team may construct the required Products in any way they see fit, as long as they deliver what is required, at the right time – they do not have to use P2.

Regular Checkpoint Reports are produced by the Team Manager from MP2 and received by the Project Manager in CS2.

Escalated Project Issues and other information will also pass from MP2 to the Project Manager, however these are received by the Project Manager in CS3 Capturing Project Issues and not CS2 Assessing Progress. The Team Manager should escalate *as soon as* they believe they cannot meet the Tolerance agreed in the Work Package.

MP3 Delivering a Completed Work Package/CS9 Accepting a Completed Work Package

Once a Work Package and its' linked Products are completed, the Project Manager is notified.

Phrases to Remember

a) A Product is not complete until it meets the quality criteria previously defined in its' Product Description.

b) The method suggests teams use P2 style plans, however they do not have to.

c) A Work Package is the *only* way to hand out work in a project.

d) A Product Description describes *what* an individual Product should look like.

e) One Work Package can refer to many Product Descriptions.

f) A Work Package defines *how* a team will work with the Project Manager.

g) The level of formality in a Work Package should be inversely proportional to the level of trust between the Project Manager and Team Manager.

h) A Work Package should state any interfaces to be recognised by the team/supplier.

4.7. Managing Stage Boundaries (SB) Process

Purpose
The purpose of the Managing Stage Boundaries (SB) process is for the Project Manager to prepare for an End Stage Assessment by the Project Board. It is invoked towards the end of a Stage to:

- update the Business Case
- update key project documents Project Plan, Risk Log, Issue Log, Lessons Learned Log
- create the Plan for the next Stage
- summarise all the above in an End Stage Report that provides options and recommendations for the future.

In addition, Managing Stage Boundaries (SB) process is invoked if the Project Board has asked for an Exception Plan to be created.

Why bother?
End Stage Assessments by the Project Board are a key Control. The Managing Stage Boundaries (SB) process is the work of the Project Manager (assisted by others as necessary), to prepare for a formal review by the Project Board. It is a key opportunity to:

- do housekeeping on key project documents
- update all the project data
- focus teams on completion of their Work Packages
- review progress and add detail to plans for the future.

Key Facts
There are 6 sub-processes in Managing Stage Boundaries (SB) process; they form 3 natural groups.

First Group – Entry points:
SB1 Planning a Stage
This is the normal entry point into SB. The next Stage Plan needs to be created.

SB6 Producing an Exception Plan
This is an alternative to SB1. This sub-process is only invoked if either the current Stage or project is forecast to finish outside of a previously agreed Tolerance, and the Project Board has requested that the Project Manager creates an Exception Plan. (An Exception Plan is just a draft Stage Plan that will be presented to the Project Board as the proposed way forward.)

Second Group – Making project information consistent:

SB2 Updating a Project Plan

Now that the details of the next Stage have been planned, various volatile parts of the Project Initiation Document (PID) need to be updated. In particular, the Project Plan, Project Approach, Project Quality Plan and Issue Log.

SB3 Updating a Project Business Case

In the method, whenever the Project Plan is updated the Business Case and Risk Log should also be updated. When Plans change the costs and time will change; this new information should be factored into the investment analysis part of the Business Case. There may also have been changes to the Business Case caused by events outside the project.

SB4 Updating the Risk Log

New Plans always change the risks in a project. Risk Analysis should be done to make sure that the correct level of risk is being taken. Plans will need to be revised to include risk countermeasures.

Third Group – Reporting end of Stage

SB5 Reporting Stage End

The Project Manager should check Configuration Management records to ensure that all the Products of the Stage are complete, and then write an End Stage Report for the Project Board and anyone else listed in the Communications Plan (created back in IP) who needs to know about the end of this Stage.

The End Stage Report should summarise and review:

- ❑ past progress
- ❑ present status, costs and quality levels
- ❑ future Plans
- ❑ the Business Case
- ❑ key risks and Project Issues
- ❑ key learning points
- ❑ options and recommendations.

Phrases to Remember

a) The Risk Log and Issue Log should, as minimum, be updated in SB.
b) An Exception Plan covers the time from 'now' until the new end of Stage date.
c) During SB you should look for any changes required to the project management team structure, in particular the people fulfilling the various roles may need to change for the next Stage. (For instance because different skills are required.)
d) It is Managing Stage Boundaries (SB) process that provides the information for a Project Board End Stage Assessment, NOT Controlling a Stage (CS) process.
e) Volatile parts of the Project Initiation Document (PID) will get updated, as minimum, during SB.
f) The Managing Stage Boundaries (SB) process will invoke the Planning (PL) process.

4.8. Closing a Project (CP) Process

Purpose
P2 covers the whole project life cycle; Closing a Project (CP) process brings the project to a controlled close *after* it has created and handed over all the required Products.

The Closing a Project (CP) process can also be invoked *before* the project has completed (premature closure). This is typically because an out of Tolerance forecast has been escalated to the Project Board, who have decided to prematurely close the project rather than carry on.

Why Bother?
The key value behind the Closing a Project (CP) process is:

- ❑ to confirm that the project really is finished before decommissioning it, e.g. don't release the staff until all Products have been accepted by their users
- ❑ to ensure that the right level of quality has been achieved overall, in addition to each individual Product meeting its' quality criteria, e.g. the final outcome must meet the customers acceptance criteria (defined back in SU) for things like ease of use, response times, reliability, factory productivity, number of defects etc
- ❑ to get sign off from management that the job is done
  e.g. getting Project Board approval
- ❑ identify any follow-on actions to be done by somebody else, e.g. outstanding Project Issues, Change Requests and risk management countermeasures
- ❑ to review project successes and failures and identify any lessons to be learned
- ❑ to plan for a future review of the project and its' outcome
- ❑ to tidy up project records and archive them
- ❑ to disband any systems and resources that are no longer needed.

Key Facts
There are only 3 sub-processes in Closing a Project Process.

CP1 Decommissioning a Project
This confirms that the Customers' Acceptance Criteria (from SU) have been met, and that operational and maintenance staff also accept that the project is complete. Project records are archived and a recommendation made to the Project Board that the project be closed.

CP2 Identifying Follow-on Actions

Recommendations for follow on actions should be made, e.g. for risk management, adoption of beneficial Change Requests, known problems etc. A Post Project Review Plan should also be created, for reviewing in the future whether the project outcome achieved the expected benefits. The Post Project Review will not take place until some time after the project finishes.

CP3 Evaluating a Project

The purpose of CP3 is to review project performance and learn any lessons. The End Project Report is written by the Project Manager, to review the whole project life cycle against expectations in the original version of the Project Initiation Document (PID) that was created back in IP. The Project Manager also reviews the contents of the Lessons Learned Log and creates a Lessons Learned Report for the Project Board. The Project Board is responsible for ensuring that any lessons to be learned are adopted elsewhere across the host organisation.

Closing a Project (CP) process is NOT in fact the last thing in a project. CP presents a set of information to the Project Board. The very last thing in a P2 project is the DP5 End Stage Assessment at which the Project Board review the information from CP and decide whether or not to allow the project to disband.

Phrases to Remember

a) The Post Project Review is planned *inside* the project but takes place *some time after* the end.

b) The End Project Report is an opportunity to review any benefits achieved *so far*, however in many projects most of the benefits will not be visible until after a period of use.

c) The DP5 End Stage Assessment takes place *after* the end of Closing a Project (CP) process.

d) Regrettably, there is no PPP (Post Project Party) defined in PRINCE2.

4.9. Planning (PL) Process

Purpose

This process describes how to make a Plan. It may be invoked at any time in a project to create any type of PRINCE2 Plan. The principle behind creating Plans is to:

- ❏ firstly define the results required from the project
- ❏ then define the activities required to achieve the desired results.

Why Bother?

Having a credible Plan is an essential pre-requisite to knowing:

- ❏ whether a business target is achievable
- ❏ how to reach a target
- ❏ what to delegate
- ❏ when to do things.

A key part of credible planning is to involve relevant user and supplier experts, thereby basing Plans on better quality information and also opening up lines of communication between suppliers, users and the Project Manager.

Never confuse activity with progress – they are different things. Being busy does not mean people are making progress; they may be busy going in the wrong direction or creating the wrong thing. Planning is all about defining the goal posts, so that activities can be very results focused.

Key Facts

The Planning (PL) process is essentially 11 steps, 4 of which are defined in the Product Based Planning technique chapter of the method.

Step 1 - PL1 Designing a Plan

This covers deciding what levels of Plan (Project, Stage or Team) to create, and is therefore closely linked to definition of Stage length (see Controls) and team structure (see Organisation). Choices of tools and policies (e.g. for planning and estimating), procedures and any special responsibilities may also need to be defined.

Step 2 - PL2 Defining and Analysing Products

This adds little in itself however invokes the 4 steps within the Product Based Planning technique:

- Step 3   Write a Product Description for the final Product
- Step 4   Draw Product Breakdown Structure
- Step 5   Write Product Descriptions (including one for the final Product)
- Step 6   Draw Product Flow Diagram

PL2 also creates the optional Product Checklist – a checklist of what Products are to be produced and their status. It's a useful alternative view to a Gantt chart.

Step 7 – PL3 Identifying Activities and Dependencies

Steps 3, 4 and 5 defined the desired *results* which the project must deliver, and documents user and supplier agreement to the quality criteria for each Product. Step 6 identifies the optimum set of activities to create each Product. This is the start of creating an activity plan or Gantt chart. Interdependencies between activities are also entered into the embryonic activity plan/Gantt chart.

Step 8 – PL4 Estimating

Estimated durations and resource requirements are added to the activity plan.

Step 9 – PL5 Scheduling

Dates on which activities should take place are added to the plan.

Step 10 – PL6 Analysing Risks

A Risk Analysis should take place and modifications made to ensure that:

- ❑   the plan contains an appropriate level of risk overall
- ❑   countermeasures are properly planned and resourced.

It may be necessary to add new activities, change resources or adjust timings to get the risk level right.

Steps 2 – 10 should be repeated as often as necessary until user, supplier and business interests agree that the plan is credible. Project Assurance can advise, Project Support can provide expertise, administrative help and leg power.

Step 11 – PL7 Completing a Plan

As well as any Gantt charts and other forms of activity plan it is necessary to provide the Project Board with:

- ❑   narrative text to justify or support the plan
- ❑   management information and corporate support systems
       e.g. resource and cashflow forecasts, budgets, time tracking systems and similar interfaces to corporate control systems.

Phrases to Remember

a) Planning is an iterative process.
b) The Project Plan is the backbone of the project.
c) All Plans have the same format and are created using the Planning (PL) process.
d) Plans must be approved by the Project Board at an End Stage Assessment *before* people start doing the activities within them.

Chapter 5.   The 3 PRINCE2 Techniques

5.1.   One Minute Overview

The 3 PRINCE2 Techniques are analogous to the skills required in making an apple pie. Skills such as peeling apples and rolling pastry have to be learned before the ingredients can be processed into an apple pie. In projects, the 3 Techniques need to be mastered so that the 8 Components can be processed into a project by following the 8 PRINCE2 Process steps.

The 3 Techniques are:

- ❑ **Product Based Planning Technique**
  A mostly visual technique for identifying the deliverables that the project must create, and what quality criteria each must meet. Users and teams/suppliers should work together to define the Products (deliverables) and their quality criteria, *before* the activities to create the Products are worked out.

- ❑ **Change Control Technique**
  This chapter of the method describes how to process Project Issues, is a little confusingly named and overlaps considerably with other modules. In *No Nonsense PRINCE2* the content of this chapter is described within the Controlling a Stage (CS) process because it is much more intuitive there.

- ❑ **Quality Review Technique**
  A way to review Products to assess whether they meet quality criteria.

5.2. Product Based Planning

Purpose

The word 'Product' is the PRINCE2 term for a deliverable. Deliverables are the results you get after completing a set of activities, e.g. a built wall, a hospital, a completed module of software or a finished document.

Product Based Planning (PBP) is a way to define what results the project is trying to achieve *before* defining the activity plan. It is analogous to deciding where the destination of a journey is *before* working out the details of how to reach it.

Product Based Planning takes place *before* the activities in a project are defined. It is an essential pre-requisite to making sure that an activity plan (or Gantt chart) is focused on delivering what the customer wants.

Product Based Planning (PBP) is a technique used within the Planning (PL) process. PBP is used within PL2 Defining and Analysing Products to identify what Products are required, *before* the activities to create those Products are defined in PL3 to PL6.

The objectives of Product Based Planning are:

- ❑ for users and suppliers to work together to define what Products (deliverables) are required from any or all of a Project, Stage or Team Plan
- ❑ to describe each Product and to negotiate quality criteria for each one
- ❑ organise all the Products into a logical sequence as a stepping stone to creating an activity plan with dependencies between tasks.

Why Bother?

The key benefits from using the Product Based Planning Technique are:

- ❑ it defines what must be delivered by each team
- ❑ the quality expectations of customer/users can be understood *before* the Product is created
- ❑ unreasonable expectations can be negotiated away
- ❑ it reveals duplicated effort
- ❑ it provides greater clarity on what activities are required
- ❑ it creates a clear link between activities, quality expectations, results and acceptance of Products
- ❑ people become more results focused
- ❑ it kick starts team work, communication and cooperation in a new plan.

Having a clear understanding of which Products a team will produce also makes it easier to empower people and delegate responsibility.

The 4 Steps in Product Based Planning
There are 4 sequential parts to Product Based Planning:

Step 1 – Write a Product Description for the Final Product of the Project
The first step is to write a Product Description that describes the final output of the project. This top level Product is essentially what the customer is paying for and what the project should aim to deliver.

Step 2 - Draw a Product Breakdown Structure (PBS)
This is a hierarchical diagram showing all the Products that must be created within a Plan, organised by meaningful grouping such as classes of Product or functional team.

Higher level groupings are broken down into increasing detail at lower levels of the PBS. The top box of a PBS always represents the completed project as defined in the Product Description written in Step 1. The second level down contains one box for each of the principal functional areas or groupings of the project – this is often a close match to the team structure. Each of the second layer boxes is then further sub-divided into the Products required within that area of the project. The principal to follow is that higher level Products in the diagram are constructed from the Products beneath them. You should use as many layers as necessary to identify *all* the Products that the project aims to produce.

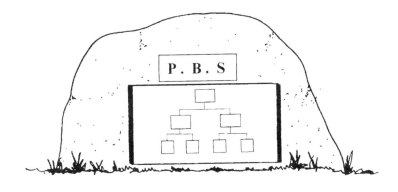

The lowest level Products in each leg are called *Simple Products* and are drawn as rectangles. Higher level Products are known as *Intermediate Products* of which there are two types – *Integration Products* and *Collective Groupings*. *Integration Products* are drawn as rectangles and are transferred to the Product Flow Diagram in step 4. *Collective Groupings* are drawn as rhomboids to illustrate the fact that they do not require work in themselves – they are just a convenient grouping such as 'Other'; they are not transferred to the Product Flow Diagram in step 4.

If a Product already exists, or is supplied as a finished item from an external source, it is known as an *External Product*. External Products are drawn as an ellipse; this is a visual clue that the Product needs to be *obtained and used* by the project, rather than *created* by the project.

The value of a Product Breakdown Structure diagram is to identify what Products must be created and/or used by the project. It is a useful brainstorming technique that results in a structured picture of the scope of a plan. It is very helpful in breaking down very large challenges into bite size chunks!

Some PBS hints and tips

a) There is no sense of time in a PBS drawing. The logical relationships between Products are added when the PBS is converted into a Product Flow Diagram (PFD).

b) The PBS identifies the fact that a Product is needed, however it does not define the characteristics that the Product must have. Expectations for Product characteristics are captured and recorded in a Product Description which should be written as soon as possible after the need for the Product is identified.

c) It is useful to identify *external* Products as ellipses rather than boxes. External Products are those Products which this project uses however is not accountable to create. External Products are often created by other projects.

d) It can be easier to draw a PBS if you define *groupings* at the first level. These are drawn as rhombi and are *not* transferred to the PFD.

e) PBS diagrams should look like the roots of a tree – splitting into more and more sub levels and not joining up with each other at lower levels.

f) Remember that Products are the *results required* e.g. a finished book, not the activities required to make the book. Product Based Planning is a technique used early in the planning work of a project. The activities required to make each Product are worked out a little later in the Planning process, *after* the nature of each Product has been defined in a Product Description and *after* the logical relationships between Products have been worked out.

f) There is an element of personal style in the way a PBS is drawn – it's not a question of being right or wrong. A good facilitator is useful to help overcome the fear of doing it wrong.

Step 3 - Write a Product Description (PD) for each Product

A Product Description is the definition of a Product, including the priceless information of:

- *who* will say when the Product is finished
- *what* quality criteria and quality expectations they wish the finished Product to meet
- *how* they will measure those criteria
- *what* skills they will use to judge.

Knowing these things means you can plan the right activities and know who to talk to about problems, changes, risks, testing and acceptance.

A PD is far more than just a form. It should be a *negotiated* agreement between user and supplier interests about what criteria the Product must meet. Writing a PD is an opportunity to set expectations at a reasonable level. It is also an excellent building block for effective communications throughout the rest of the project.

Once agreed, a PD is used (as part of a Work Package) to inform team managers about what results they must achieve. The quality criteria and methods defined within the PD can then form the basis of tests to confirm whether the Product presented by the team meets the required criteria. A key point of the method is that a Product is not complete until it meets the criteria defined in the relevant Product Description.

It is mandatory to have Product Descriptions for the top level Product of the project and each of the lowest level *Simple Products*.

Step 4 - Draw a Product Flow Diagram (PFD)
This diagram is a conversion of the Product Breakdown Structure. The only new information to add is the logical relationships between Products.

A PFD is constructed by rearranging the Products within the PBS into logical end-to-end relationships. Arrows from one Product to another show logical relationships and time flowing either from top to bottom or left to right. Inevitably the top box of a PBS will be the 'last' box on a PFD.

Collective Grouping Products are *not* transferred from product Breakdown Structure into the Product Flow Diagram.

A Product Flow Diagram will reveal parallel and sequential threads of Products, e.g. 'walls' must come after 'foundations' and before 'roof', however foundation, walls and roof can be worked on in parallel to 'swimming pool' and 'helicopter landing pad'. Such logical relationships are not always obvious; working them out is a useful way to get an early overview of the Plan.

Natural Stage boundaries often align with nodal points in the PFD, where many parallel threads merge together and then split again.

What happens after a PFD is completed?
After Product Based Planning has been completed (top level PD, PBS, PDs, PFD), you should return to the Planning (PL) process and do PL3 Identifying Activities and Dependencies.

In PL3 experts work out what activities are needed to construct each Product; this is the starting point for creating a project activity plan or Gantt chart.

5.3. Change Control Technique

The method describes the various aspects of Change Control in several different chapters, much of it within the context of handling Project Issues.

The Change Control Technique chapter covers how Project Issues should be processed.

It is most intuitive to consider Project Issue handling within Controlling a Stage (CS) process, which is why this chapter of the PRINCE2 manual is not described here.

Please refer to CS3 Capturing Project Issues and CS4 Examining Project Issues.

5.4. Quality Review Technique

Purpose

The Quality Review technique is a suggested way to review a document to assess whether it meets the quality criteria agreed previously in the relevant Product Description. (The technique works fine with any Product, not just documents).

The key purpose of Quality Review is to establish whether a Product is fit for purpose or not.

Why Bother:
Teams/suppliers must prove that their Products are complete before handing a completed Work Package back to the Project Manager. Holding a Quality Review with the users who set the quality criteria for the Product is one way to confirm that the Product is finished.

Successful completion of a Quality Review could be linked to a payment milestone for a supplier. Interim Quality Reviews can be scheduled if there are doubts about the quality of a Product, or a third party supplier is not trusted.

The project is finished when all the Products are proved to be complete.

Key Facts

A Quality Review is a planned activity. The Chairperson and reviewers should be chosen at Stage planning time.

The three steps in performing a Quality Review are *Preparation, Review Meeting* and *Follow-up*. They work well like this:

Preparation
- ❑ the Chairperson decides whether the Product is ready for review or not
- ❑ the Producer sends the Product and its' Product Description to the Reviewers
- ❑ reviewers review the Product and feed back errors to the Producer; this should be done against a previously agreed Product Description
- ❑ the Producer fixes any minor errors

Review Meeting
- ❑ if there are significant errors a meeting can be held to decide on responsibilities for fixing the situation

Follow-up
- ❑ the Producer makes the necessary changes and gets them approved by individual reviewers
- ❑ the Chairperson can decide whether actions from the meeting are complete

Phrases to Remember

a) Quality Review can happen at any time, not just at the end of a Stage.

b) The 'scribe' role takes the minutes of any meetings.

c) Project Assurance can chair reviews, advise on participants and be reviewers themselves.

d) A Product that does not meet the quality criteria within its' Product Description is known as an Off-Specification Product.

e) An Off-Specification Product should be handled as a Project Issue.

f) Only the Project Board may accept an Off-Specification Product; this is called a Concession.

g) The Chairman and Reviewers are chosen at Stage planning time.

h) The PRINCE2 manual was not written to be humorous, however one piece of light relief escaped onto P.307. *"The aim of the quality review is to identify defects in the Product not in the Producer."*

Chapter 6.   Key Cross-Topic Themes

The PRINCE2 manual is structured to explain each of the modules one by one, organised into major sections describing:

- ❑ Processes
- ❑ Components
- ❑ Technique
- ❑ Appendices

The manual contains a lot of valuable information about what each module is, why it is important and how it might be tailored to suit different requirements. The downside of this structure is that cross-topic themes and the way the processes link together over time are hard to piece together, especially for those new to the method or who are in a hurry. It can be necessary to consult 7 or more chapters to understand how a thematic timeline such as Exception Handling works.

To help people new to the method, the following sections bring together aspects of many different chapters from the method to provide focused explanations of the following important themes:

- ❑ Key Theme 1 - The PRINCE2 timeline
  How the 8 Processes, 8 Components, 3 Techniques and Appendices fit together and are used over the whole project lifecycle. This is described using a simple, fictitious, boat building project as an example.

- ❑ Key Theme 2 – Working with Teams and Supplier
  How to work with teams/suppliers throughout the project lifecycle.

- ❑ Key Theme 3 - Handling Project Issues and Change Requests
  How to process Project Issues and ensure that fact based decisions are taken by the right people at the right time.

- ❑ Key Theme 4 - Exception Handling
  What the Project Manager should do *as soon as* they believe the Stage or project is going to finish outside of a previously agreed Tolerance.

6.1. Key Theme 1 - The PRINCE2 Timeline

The PRINCE2 manual is organised into 30 standalone chapters that describe each module in turn. People new to the method usually struggle to piece together all the separate modules into a timeline.

The following section outlines the typical timeline order of events in a PRINCE2 project. You may want to refer to the fish diagram at the back of the book – this shows the processes and individual documents against the timeline and Stages.

The project is to build a boat, and is expected to last around 12 months. It's a big boat!

The People Involved
This project involves the following people.

You
You are the Project Manager.

Mrs Major
Your boss. She wants the new boat, and will pay all the bills. She is a very busy person, runs a hat factory and is often out of the country.

Aima Helper
Mrs Major's secretary. She has offered to provide secretarial and administrative help. She is also a financial expert and will look after the project finances.

Jack Smiler
This is the Customer Service Manager from Boats-R-Us. He does all their sales work and is responsible for making sure customer orders are reasonable, achievable and then fulfilled.

Bob Boatbuilder
A skilled foreman of the Boats-R-Us company. Bob and his team will build the main structure of the boat, however they will not do the internal fittings.

Ivor Chisel
A wood carver who will install all the internal wooden fittings, and will carve pictures into the woodwork. Mrs Major knows Ivor – he did a nice job on her kitchen cabinets last year.

Archie Tekt

This is a friend of Mrs Major - he has a lot of experience of building customised boats. He has offered to keep a watchful eye on the project for Mrs Major whilst she is away on business.

Week 1 Getting started

Mrs Major decides to run a project to build her new dream boat. She tells you to organise everything and gives you the brochure from Boats-R-Us. *"I want a boat like that"* she says, *"plus a few extras."* This is the only information in your Project Mandate. You decide to run the Project along PRINCE2 lines.

SU1   Mrs Major agrees she is the Project Executive, and she appoints you as the Project Manager.

SU2   You identify the various stakeholders and decide who you want to ask to take a role in the project management team. There are not very many people in this project, so combining many of the 9 management roles is sensible.

You decide you would like:
- ❏   Mrs Major to be Senior User as well as Executive
- ❏   Jack Smiler to be the Senior Supplier
- ❏   Mrs Major says she wants Archie Tekt to do all 3 Project Assurance roles
- ❏   Aima Helper will provide Project Support
- ❏   Bob Boatbuilder and Ivor Chisel will both be Team Managers.

SU3   You go and talk to all the people involved and negotiate and agree their project roles. The external people want written role descriptions, which you provide.

SU4   Having talked to people over the last few days you now have an outline understanding of what the project is about. You write the Project Brief (only about 2 sides of paper) and create the Risk Log, Daily Log and Outline Business Case. An obvious risk is that Mrs Major has not said what *"a few extras"* means. You do some Risk Analysis and record some countermeasures in the Risk Log. The main countermeasure is to get Mrs Major to define what extras she wants as part of the Project Brief including the Customers Quality Expectations.

SU5   The general strategy for the project will be to get the basic boat built, sail it round to the local marina, then get Ivor Chisel to finish the interior. You write a Project Approach, however as it is only a couple of paragraphs long you make it a section within the Project Brief.

SU6   Mrs Major wants to see a PID for the whole one year project; you estimate it will take a couple of weeks to produce the PID and during that couple of weeks all the key stakeholders will need to attend various workshops and do various activities. You write a short Plan (draft Initiation Stage Plan) for Mrs Major that shows what everyone will be doing over the next few weeks and the various activities needed to produce the PID.

DP1   Mrs Major and the other Project Board members review the Project Brief, Project Approach and draft Initiation Stage Plan. They like them, they don't think the risks are too high, and they decide to commit the resources to do an IP stage during which the project will be planned in detail. You agree to present detailed costs and plans to them 2 weeks from today, plus or minus 2 days Tolerance.

Weeks 2–4 Defining details

You spend the next 2 weeks running the IP Stage. This involves negotiating and agreeing a variety of different things with Project Board members and the specialist technical teams. You start to create all the different pieces of information that will ultimately be assembled into a Project Initiation Document (PID). A lot of this information is easy to obtain – things like policies and procedures already exist. Other information needs more effort, such as quality criteria for key Products and details of activities.

You work on the following key areas at this time.

IP1   You write a brief Project Quality Plan that states procedures, policies, responsibilities, tools, quality checking arrangements etc for ensuring the boat ends up meeting Mrs Major's requirements. You also decide to write a separate Stage Quality Plan for each stage, stating the specific quality checking arrangements for each of the different Stages of the project. Different quality control skills will be required when building the boat and testing it at sea. You make a note in your Daily Log to write the Stage Quality Plan for the sea trials later in the project when you understand more about how to do the testing.

IP2   You need to plan as much of the project as is visible at this time. You don't have to plan all the details right through to the end, just the details of the next Stage and an outline of the remainder of the project.

You need to define the deliverables required in the project, and the activities to create each deliverable. You follow the Planning (PL) process to work this information out.

>   **PL1**   Since this is a small project you decide to have a Project Plan and not to have separate Stage Plans. Each supplier will have their own Team Plans; you will only track the key dates and deliverables of the teams.

>   **PL2**   You hold a workshop with Archie Tekt, Bob Boatbuilder and Ivor Chisel and together create a Product Breakdown Structure, Product Descriptions for each Product (including the final Product), and a Product Flow Diagram. During the workshop you realise that Ivor Chisel is only expecting to carve the doors, he is not expecting to fit all the other internal fittings such as a cocktail cabinet and leather chairs. It takes all day but now everyone is much clearer about what they need to produce. A team spirit is starting to develop, so you all go for a drink in the local pub.

>   **PL3**   The day after the workshop everybody that is responsible for a Product starts to create an activity plan defining what work has to be done, who will do it, how long it will take (**PL4**), and when it will take place (**PL5**). You have to renegotiate with the Jack Smiler from Boats-R-Us for them to do the extra fitting out work.

>   After a few days you combine all this information into one Project Plan; you have to negotiate key dates and dependencies with the teams as everyone has assumed different things.

Four natural decision points are starting to appear:
1. end of IP
2. end of building the basic boat
3. end of wood carving
4. end of sea trials.

You define 4 Stages around these decision points. You decide not to have a formal closure Stage.

PL6 You look at the risks in the plan and decide to allow a few extra days between completion of the basic boat and commencement of interior fitting out.

PL7 Now that all the costs are known, the Project Plan can be completed by adding cashflow forecasts, staff requirements and a few words to explain why the plan is the way it is, e.g. why Ivor Chisel will be doing less work than originally expected.

IP3 Since the Plans, costs and risks are now known, you can finalise the Business Case. Aima Helper does an investment appraisal and compares various options for how Mrs Major can finance the project. Working closely with Archie Tekt you analyse the key risks listed in the Risk Log and work out what to do about them.

IP4 You have a conversation with Mrs Major about what reports, Stages and other Controls she would like. You agree to provide a weekly summary Highlight Report on a Friday afternoon that you will email to the Project Board members and Archie Tekt. She agrees on the length of the Stages and expected dates of Project Board meetings.

You consider whether to write a separate Communications Plan or not. This would be a definition of how the various suppliers will keep in touch with the project, each other and you. This is a small project so you just create a list of phone numbers and give it to everyone involved. You tell them all to contact each other once a week and whenever they have any queries or concerns.

IP5 You ask Aima Helper how to set up a project filing system to store electronic and paper documents. She tells you that she did it for you 2 weeks ago and was wondering why you were the only person not using it. She tells you all the other administrative and support things she can help you with too – it's a long list and will allow you to spend more time on higher value project management tasks.

IP6 Now that the plans and ideas have settled down and the key stakeholders are happy, you assemble the Project Initiation Document (PID) from all the separate parts that already exist. The Next Stage Plan is also created using **SB1**.

DP2 The Project Board reviews the PID. They like it and decide to go ahead and place the orders for the work to commence. They approve your plan and give you authority to execute that plan plus or minus two weeks, and plus or minus 10% of cost.

Weeks 5-20 Building the Boat Stage
CS1 You start kicking off the activities in the plan by negotiating Work Packages with Bob Boatbuilder and Ivor Chisel, agreeing key dates and placing contracts where

necessary. You agree with both of them that they will email you a summary Checkpoint Report on a Thursday afternoon. You also agree Tolerance and escalation processes with them – they will phone you as soon as they forecast more than 1 day deviation in time or 2% of cost.

CS2 Late on each Thursday afternoon you read the Checkpoint Reports and update the Stage Plan, Issue Log and Risk Log with the data they contain. Work is progressing nicely.

CS5 You review what all the new data means and decide that the Stage is broadly on schedule. Some things are a bit behind schedule, others are a bit ahead.

Week 11
Bob Boatbuilder telephones you one morning in Week 11. He tells you that there has been a mistake and the boat is 25 centimetres shorter than it should be. Oops! You log this as a Project Issue (**CS3**).

You examine the Project Issue (**CS4**) and are not sure what the full impact will be, so you ask for help from Archie Tekt (Project Assurance). Archie thinks the change in specification might be quite significant, so you ask various experts to do an impact assessment. Jack Smiler from Boats-R-Us is closely involved with the impact assessment because he is responsible for all boat building work and it is his people who have made the mistake. The experts decide that one of the storage cupboards will have to be made smaller, but it's not too much of a problem. Jack Smiler agrees to pay for the extra work because his people made the mistake.

You consider what this problem means to the Stage and project (**CS5**); since you're not sure how big a problem this is you ask Archie Tekt what he recommends. Together you decide to amend the activities slightly (**CS7**); the completion dates and costs of the Stage will not be affected.

In **week 18** you start to prepare for the End Stage Assessment in 2 weeks time. You spend time focussing on completing the Products of the current Stage, updating the plans with actual progress to date, tidying up all the project records and making sure everything is going to finish within Tolerance. You also start to use the SB process to create plans for the next Stage.

Key aspects of preparing for the next End Stage Assessment by Mrs Major are:

- ❑ SB1 Plan the next Stage in detail
- ❑ SB2 Update the Project Plan
- ❑ SB3 Update the Business Case once more detail about the future dates and costs is worked out in SB1 and SB2
- ❑ SB4 Update the Risk Log with new risks and their countermeasures

Week 20
The Stage is ending this week so you summarise the past, present, future, key issues, key risks, Business Case and options in an End Stage Report to Mrs Major and the other Project Board members.

The Project Board review your next Stage Plan, Business Case, key risks and overall Project Plan at an End Stage Assessment (**DP3**). Things are going OK, Mrs Major is confident she has the money to pay for the boat, so they are happy to commit funds to the next Stage. Mrs Major thinks the next Stage is going to be more risky than previous ones, so she narrows your Tolerance to plus or minus one week, plus or minus 5% of cost, and any 'significant' changes to the specification. You think that the word 'significant' is a bit vague; you discuss this with Mrs Major however she says she trusts you to 'do the right thing'.

Week 21
A busy week! You start running the new plan; there are lots of new Work Packages to agree with the teams, and lots of things to check out and arrange. Aima Helper does a lot of the legwork for you.

Week 24
Bad news this week! The specialist fitter, Ivor Chisel, goes sick and won't be back for at least a month. You log this as an Issue **(CS3)** and do a quick impact analysis **(CS4)**. You know this is going to delay the project beyond the time Tolerance previously agreed with Mrs Major, so you immediately escalate the problem by telephoning her and make a verbal Exception Report to her that the project is unexpectedly in Exception. You both discuss the facts and options. She does not want to prematurely close the project; she asks you to come back in a few days with a new plan.

You spend the next few days preparing an Exception Plan **(SB6)**. You find a new fitter that can fit out the interior of the boat, however they can't do the carving. You discuss this with Mrs Major; she decides to have the carving done once Ivor Chisel gets back to work, and doesn't mind waiting a few months as long as the rest of the boat is ready on schedule. This would mean that the wood carving Stage gets dropped, thereby allowing the sea trials to be run a few weeks earlier.

Now that the way forward is clear you update the plans, Business Case and risks **(SB3, SB4, SB5)** and present the new plans to the Project Board at their Exception Assessment **(DP3)**. The Exception Plan shows that the boat will be ready (except for the carving) in week 40, earlier than originally thought. The carving will be done by a different project that will follow on soon after this one finishes.

The Project Board approve the Exception Plan – it becomes your new Stage Plan.

Weeks 25 – 40
The remaining weeks go very smoothly. Team Managers provide you with Checkpoint Reports on Wednesday afternoons, and you create Highlight Reports at the regular intervals Mrs Major requested. Stage boundaries come and go; there are few big surprises and no muddle. Everyone says how much easier it is to do good work when you know what results are required.

Weeks 41-45
It's getting towards the end of the project now and testing is going very well. One by one the various Products were completed and tested. The user manual for the online cocktail cabinet failed a Quality Review, however with a little bit of re-work and overtime by Boats-R-Us it was corrected.

In week 41 you are Reviewing Stage Status **(CS5)** and decide to trigger the formal closure of the project. You notify people of the imminent end of the project, and tell them you are going to do a formal closure because there are a lot of payments depending on customer acceptance.

Formal Closure

You are expecting final acceptance of the boat go very smoothly. Throughout the project the Boats-R-Us team have been using the Product Descriptions for the key deliverables to check that the features of the boat match the expectations agreed with the users. When they were not sure, they checked the Product Description to find out who was going to do the acceptance testing and then talked to them.

CP1   Final customer acceptance was easy because throughout the project you had ensured that suppliers worked closely with users to define what results were required. Whenever there were problems the effective communications made it easy to work out what to do. Operational and maintenance acceptance was easy to get; the boat maintenance crew said thankyou for listening to their ideas way back in the early weeks of the project.

You archive copies of key project records, supplier contracts and technical designs so that they can be easily found and used again by other projects. Mrs Major asked you to be particularly careful to archive all the financial information – she is expecting a visit from the Tax Inspector!

CP2   There are some outstanding actions that you need to handover to the boat crew, so you write down Follow On Action Recommendations. These include a note to remember to apply for a certificate of sea worthiness when the current temporary one expires, and there are some minor change requests to be analysed. There's a risk that the cocktail cabinet won't be big enough for some of Mrs Major's parties, so you hand over your ideas on mitigating actions. The carving hasn't yet been finished, so you hand over all the details of what has to be done.

Mrs Major wants to review the project formally in a few months time, after she has enjoyed using the boat for her summer holiday in the sun. You make a Post Project Review Plan and give it to Aima Helper to add to Mrs Major's diary.

CP3   In week 45 you write an End Project Report summarising what happened in the project and explaining the deviations from the original PID signed off back in week 4 by the Project Board. You have been keeping a log of any lessons to be learned as the project progressed, and you now write this up formally into a Lessons Learned Report. Some of the lessons are technical, others are to do with project management processes and working with subcontractors. You give the Lessons Learned Report to Mrs Major to help her make the next project even better.

Mrs Major was so happy with her new boat that she invited everybody to a party on board. Ivor Chisel was feeling much better; he came along to measure up for the carving work. Mrs Major said she had a lot of confidence in your abilities and wanted you to project manage the relocation of her hat factory to Spain next summer. She said you could use the boat as a hotel and office for a few months…….

6.2. Key Theme 2 – Working with Teams and Suppliers

PRINCE2 handles both in-house teams and external suppliers in exactly the same way. Choices must be made on the level of formality and documentation required, based on the level of trust between the parties.

Since the Project Manager has the authority to adjust the Stage Plan within Tolerance (CS7), they must also be responsible for deciding when team/supplier work must start and finish, otherwise it would be chaotic.

Tolerance is usually defined in terms of time and cost, however tolerances on scope, quality, risk and benefit may be relevant.

Giving work to teams/suppliers uses:

- ❑ Work Packages
  A negotiated contract between Project Manager and Team Manager agreeing how they will work together:
      - which Products the team will create
      - key milestone dates and costs
      - reporting arrangements, interfaces and escalation
      - completion criteria.

- ❑ Product Descriptions
  Detailed definitions of individual deliverables. In particular:
      - what the Product is
      - who will accept the finished Product (should be a user)
      - the criteria the users want the Product to meet
      - the method the users will use to assess whether the Product meets the stated criteria.

Product Descriptions are part of a Plan and will have been previously agreed by the Project Board at the previous End Stage Assessment.

Team Managers and subject experts within the teams will have been involved in planning a Stage, and will frequently develop Team Plans in parallel with the Stage or Project Plan. Teams do NOT have to use PRINCE2.

The Senior Supplier(s) will have committed the resources necessary for their teams to create the planned Products, and will have agreed that the Plan is realistic and achievable. Project Assurance from the supplier perspective can advise the Project Manager and assure the Senior Supplier that the supplier interests are being handled in an appropriate way.

The Project Manager (CS1 Authorising a Work Package) negotiates a Work Package with a Team Manager (MP1 Accepting a Work Package). Ideally, long pieces of technical work should be divided up into Work Packages that align with End Stage Assessments by the Project Board (DP3).

The Team Managers manage the creation of the required Products (MP2 Executing a Work Package), and send Checkpoint Reports to the Project Manager (received in CS2 Assessing Progress) on a regular time basis agreed in the Work Package.

During MP2 the Team Manager must prove that Product(s) are complete by demonstrating that they meet the quality criteria previously set by the users in the Product Description(s). The Quality Review technique is one of many ways to do this. Other ways might include:

- ❑ user trials
- ❑ testing
- ❑ independent scrutiny
- ❑ judgement of experts.

The Quality Log (previously created in IP) will contain details of expected and actual quality checking activities. The Team Manager must update the Quality Log with actual events and results; this is to allow easy audit and assurance that quality standards are being maintained.

In CS2 the Project Manager should update the Stage Plan with actual progress to date, and Risk Log and Issue Log updates may be required. Guidance and information may of course be passed from the Project Manager to the Team Manager. Earned Value Analysis might be used to assess progress of a team, however this only gets a passing reference in the manual.

Highlight Reports should be sent (CS6 Reporting Highlights) to the Project Board (DP4), including the Senior Supplier and anyone else defined in the Communications Plan, at a time frequency and content agreed with the Project Board at the previous End Stage Assessment.

The Team Manager must assess progress of their work during MP2. As soon as they feel that out of Tolerance completion of their Work Package is likely they must escalate this Exception condition to the Project Manager. This would be done by raising an Issue.

The Project Manager should Review Stage Status (CS5) frequently. Day to day events will inevitably deviate from the Stage Plan. Very small deviations may not require any reaction. More significant deviations will require the Project Manager to Take Corrective Action (CS7), e.g. changing dates or even adding new Work Packages. This is OK as long as the Project Manager believes the Stage will still complete within previously agreed Tolerances.

As soon as the Project Manager starts to forecast that the Stage or project will not complete within Tolerance they have lost their authority to proceed and MUST do CS8 Escalating Project Issues.

In CS8 the Project Manager raises an Exception Report stating what has happened, the impact on Plans, Business Case and risks, and early views on options and recommendations. This is received by the Project Board including the Senior Supplier(s) who represent line management from the teams and suppliers. The Project Board then decides how to proceed - this is explained in Exception Handling.

Change Requests, Project Issues and risks will of course affect teams; elements of the method will be used to report, escalate and pass down decisions. In particular:

- ❑ Checkpoint Reports
- ❑ Highlight Reports
- ❑ Off-Specification Products and Concessions.

Once a team has proved in MP2 that all Products within a Work Package are complete, the completed Work Package is handed back by the Team Manager (MP3 Delivering a Completed Work Package) to the Project Manager (CS9 Accepting a Completed Work Package).

Any learning points should be captured into the Lessons Learned Log and summarised in the End Stage Report. The Senior Supplier(s) should share these with the teams and suppliers.

During Closing a Project (CP) process, the Project Manager should write an End Project Report (CP3) summarising amongst other things the handling of teams and suppliers, including a review of actual events compared against original expectations set in the Project Initiation Document (PID) created back in IP.

The Follow-on Action Recommendations created in CP2 may include outstanding risk or Project Issue management actions affecting teams/suppliers. The Senior Supplier(s) should ensure effective handover when the teams are decommissioned.

6.3.   Key Theme 3 - Handling Issues and Change Requests

PRINCE2 uses a clearly defined set of concepts and steps (called Project Issue handling) to formally handle problems and Change Requests. The objective is to ensure that all such matters are handled:

- ❑ in a timely manner
- ❑ by the appropriate people
- ❑ based on the facts.

Decisions should be made by people at the appropriate level, based on what is best for the business as a whole and the Tolerance they have previously been given.

The Project Board may choose to define:

- ❑ a Change Authority role
  One or more people empowered to make decisions about change on behalf of the Project Board.

- ❑ a Change Budget
  A budget for time and/or money for the Change Authority to spend. The budget can be for any single change and/or all change in a Stage.

Project Assurance from user, supplier and business perspectives should be consulted if there is any doubt about the impact of a Project Issue or how it should be processed.

Anyone may raise a Project Issue however the Project Manager is responsible for day to day processing of them. Since Project Issue handling is a formal process it should not be used for day to day trivial matters.

There are different types of Project Issue, all of which are handled in the same way:

- ❑ **Statements of concern, questions and new information**
  Any statement of concern or problem. E.G. a team/supplier delivering late, or loss of a key team member, or new information that needs to be formally tracked.

- ❑ **Off-Specifications**
  This is the term for a Product (deliverable) that does not meet the quality criteria that users and suppliers have previously agreed as being required and achievable. (Quality criteria for a Product are defined in its' Product Description.)

- ❑ **Requests for Change**
  Requests from either users or suppliers to modify something previously agreed. E.G. "Can we have it pink and not blue?"

PRINCE2 suggests 5 different priorities of Change Request:

1. Must have
2. Important
3. Nice to have
4. Cosmetic and not important
5. Not a change

The steps in Project Issue handling are as follows.

Step 1 - CS3 Capturing Project Issues
The Project Issue should be captured and logged in the Issue Log that was set up during IP. A confirmation of receipt should be sent to the originator. Project Support can help.

Step 2 - CS4 Examining Project Issues
The Project Manager should make an early assessment of the priority and urgency of the new Project Issue. If in doubt, ask Project Assurance.

An impact assessment must be done on the Project Issue to establish the impact on current Stage Plan, Project Plan, Business Case, risks and other Project Issues. It is important to involve users and suppliers in impact assessment. Project Assurance roles from user, supplier and business interests are likely to be involved because they have wisdom in such matters.

The facts about the impact of the Project Issue should be added to the Issue Log. The priority may need to be revised during impact assessment.

If the Project Issue is a Change Request, it is important to assess whether the Change Request is beneficial or not. A beneficial Change Request is one where the increase in benefit (e.g. reduced project costs or increased functionality), significantly exceeds the impact in terms of extra cost, delays or increased risk.

Step 3 - CS5 Reviewing Stage Status
CS5 is like the analytical part of the Project Manager's brain. CS4 gathers facts about the Project Issue, CS5 analyses the impact of those facts on the current Stage Plan, Project Plan, Business Case and risks.

In CS5 the Project Manager must decide about the Project Issue. Options are:

- do nothing because the Project Issue has gone away or has no impact
- reject the Change Request because it is not beneficial
- CS6 Reporting Highlights
  Seek the opinion of the Project Board via a Highlight Report
- CS7 Take Corrective Action
  make minor adjustments to the Stage Plan to address a Project Issue or implement a Change Request
- CS8 Escalate Project Issues
  escalate to the Project Board any Project Issues whose impacts lead you to forecast that either Stage or Project tolerances can no longer be achieved.

Previous Highlight Reports (via CS6) may have given early warning of these problems.

The Project Manager has no authority to change Approved Products (deliverables completed in a previous Stage). All such decisions must be taken by the Project Board, who would be informed of the need to make a decision via an Exception Report created by the Project Manager in CS8 Escalating Project Issues.

An Exception Report is the mechanism for informing the Project Board of the need to make any type of decision that is beyond the Project Manager's authority. There's nothing wrong with verbal Exception Reports where appropriate, however greater formality and an audit trail are desirable if there is a serious threat to Tolerance.

Step 4 – Change Plans and Products
If a Change Request is to be adopted, there will need to be changes to Product Descriptions, Plans, activities, configuration management records as well as the affected Products themselves.

A major change might trigger Exception handling, although this would normally be picked up in CS4 or CS5 when examining the impact of the Change Request or Project Issue.

6.4.   Key Theme 4 - Exception Handling

The decision making authority of the Project Manager is to execute the Plan for a Stage within the 6 types of Tolerance previously agreed with the Project Board. It is similar for Team Managers however they only have authority over Work Packages. Project Managers and Team Managers must escalate and seek new instructions *as soon as* they believe that any of the 6 Tolerances cannot be met. This may occur because of a major new Project Issue, or an accumulation of too many smaller ones. Exception handling is the decision making process to handle this situation.

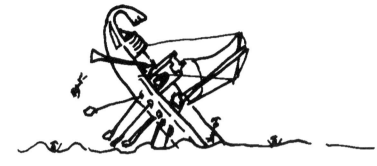

Previous Highlight Reports sent from Project Manager (CS6 Reporting Highlights) to Project Board (received in DP4 Giving Ad-hoc Direction) may have given early warning.

The cause of the Exception should have been logged as a Project Issue (CS3 Capturing Project Issues) and examined (CS4 Examining Project Issues) which will have revealed the forecast out of Tolerance condition (CS5 Reviewing Stage Status).

The Project Manager uses CS8 Escalating Project Issues to inform the Project Board (DP4 Giving Ad-hoc Direction). It is courteous and sensible to verbally inform the Project Board before formal escalation. The Project Manager (in CS8 Escalating Project Issues) writes an Exception Report for the Project Board, stating:

- ❑   what the problem is
- ❑   the impact of the problem on Business Case, Plans, risks
- ❑   any immediately obvious options for what to do next
- ❑   the impact of each option on Business Case, Plans, risks
- ❑   the Project Manager's recommendations.

The Project Board receive the Exception Report in DP4 Giving Ad-hoc Direction and decide what to do next. They have several options:

❑ Reject it, hold it pending, fix the cause

❑ Premature Closure
   Stop the project immediately because there is no benefit in continuing. They may wish to execute the Closing a Project (CP) process (called Premature Closure) to ensure an orderly disembarkation from the sinking ship.

❑ Request an Exception Plan
   Ask the Project Manager to create an Exception Plan to define any activities

required through to the new end of Stage. This will require some replanning and might take weeks or even months before the Exception Plan is ready for review.

The option chosen by the Project Board will depend on the cause of the Exception, the strength of the Business Case, new time and cost estimates, and general level of risk.

If the Project Board want to re-plan the remainder of the Stage, the Project Manager creates an Exception Plan using a combination of Managing Stage Boundaries (SB) process and the Planning (PL) process as follows:

- ❑ SB6 Producing an Exception Plan
  This sub-process invokes the Planning (PL) process and, if necessary, the Product Based Planning technique to create a new Plan to correct the Exception condition from now until the new end of this Stage.

- ❑ SB2 Updating a Project Plan
  The Project Plan will need updating as well because frequently exception conditions lead to delays to project completion.

- ❑ SB3 - Updating a Project Business Case
  Whenever the Plans are updated the Business Case must also be updated because it contains:
    - a summary of timescales and costs
    - an Investment Analysis which will need updating if costs and time have changed
    - new risks may need to be reviewed by the Project Board.

- ❑ SB4 - Updating the Risk Log
  The risks will have changed so a new Risk Analysis should be performed and the Risk Log updated.

- ❑ SB5 - Reporting Stage End
  The Project Manager should present the Exception Plan to the Project Board. A summary may be required in the format of an End Stage Report.

The Project Board review the Exception Plan at an Exception Assessment (DP3 Authorising a Stage or Exception Plan) which is the same as a normal End Stage Assessment except that it is not at the end of a Stage. As usual, the Project Board only has three basic options:

- ❑ Premature Closure
  Stop the project because there is no benefit in continuing.

- ❑ Proceed as planned
  The Exception Plan replaces the current Stage Plan.

- ❑ Redirect
  The Exception Plan is not yet acceptable and needs further work.

Judgement and Project Board guidance is needed when deciding how much project work should continue between writing an Exception Report and reviewing an Exception Plan.

Chapter 7.   Top 10 Tips on Passing the Exams

The APM Group Ltd administer a professional examination system on behalf of OGC. Thousands of people every year sit the Foundation and Practitioner exams to prove their understanding of PRINCE2. The qualification is widely accepted internationally, and is becoming more and more important in the public and private sector job markets.

There are 2 levels of examination:

- **Foundation**

  This is a one hour, closed book, multiple choice exam with 75 questions. It tests understanding of the method and terminology. All the answers are documented within the official manual. The global average pass rate is around 97%.

- **Practitioner**

  This is a three hour, open book, written exam, in which a simple project scenario is given to candidates, who then have to answer a series of questions about how PRINCE2 would be applied. Answers need to demonstrate an understanding of how the method works, AND how it applies to the situation presented. The global average pass rate is around 67%. You can take any materials into the exam, including *No Nonsense PRINCE2,* as long as they are not electronic!

The pass mark for both exams is to score 50% or more. You must pass the Foundation exam before entering for the Practitioner. The Practitioner result is valid for 5 years, after which it must be renewed via a short refresh test.

7.1. Top 10 Foundation Exam Tips

Tip 1. All questions are based on phrases or key points in the official manual, so the more you have studied the manual the better. *No Nonsense PRINCE2* uses key phrases from the official manual, many of which are also the basis of Foundation questions.

Tip 2. Practice makes perfect. Sample exams are available from Accredited Training Organisations. Practice the sample exams until you have learned the right answers and picked up on various important subtleties in the method.

Tip 3. Be realistic!!! You've only got to get half marks to pass. Put away your personal pride and allow yourself to get some wrong. Many of the questions will be probing points of detail rather than fundamental concepts; you can afford to get quite a few wrong without feeling that you don't understand the method.

Tip 4. Some of the questions will ask which answer is FALSE, or which answer is NOT true. Leave these until last; answer easier questions first and come back to these later in the exam. To answer them, invert the question and eliminate any answer that is true. E.G., if the question is ……….

> *Question x: Which of the following is NOT defined in PRINCE2?*
> *a) The Daily Log*   *b) The Daily Newspaper*
> *c) Highlight Report*   *c) Risk Log*

…….. ask yourself "Is it TRUE that the Daily Log is defined in PRINCE2?" If it *is* true, then cross out (a) because it cannot be the answer to the question. Hopefully this will eliminate 3 options; the 4th must be NOT true and therefore is the right answer. Phew!! (It's easy to get these wrong, so see Tip 3).

Tip 5. If you don't know an answer, eliminate any options that you know are wrong. This will increase your chance of guessing correctly. Eliminate any options that don't sound PRINCE2-like, then take a guess.

Tip 6. There are NO weekly or monthly meetings or reports in the method, so don't choose an answer with the words 'weekly' or 'monthly' in it.

Tip 7. Check that you have answered EVERY question. It is ALWAYS worth a guess. It is surprising how many candidates do not answer every question and miss out on a mark or two.

Tip 8. Once you have finished your paper get up and leave the room (although you're not supposed to leave in the last 15 minutes.) People who sit there fiddling with their answers usually lose more marks than they gain.

Tip 9. Normally the Foundation paper is marked by the Trainer, and you get the results straight after the exam. If you fail you can resit on the same day after some more tuition.

Tip 10. If you get extremely nervous before exams, you can help yourself by practicing exam questions in the week before the Foundation exam. Many of the freely available sample questions are very similar, or even identical, to live questions. The more you practice the more questions you will learn to recognise and answer correctly.

7.2. Top 10 Practitioner Exam Tips

Tip 1. A key reason for people failing is bad time management. The papers are very carefully tested by the APM Group to make sure candidates can answer them in the time available. Follow the rule that *marks equals minutes*. If a question is worth 40 marks, work on it for 40 minutes and then STOP and move onto the next question. If you do this you will have attempted all the questions and have around 30 minutes contingency time for coffee, toilet, extra work on questions you have not answered well etc. If you spend 2 hours answering a 40 mark question you cannot possibly get more than 40 marks, and will probably fail the exam.

Tip 2. Answer the question the examiner asked. In particular, look for key words such as *how, what, when.* It is surprising how many candidates write good responses to the wrong question. For instance, if the question is "Explain how Highlight Reports are used", some candidates will create a competent Highlight Report. Unfortunately this will gain few marks because they have not provided an explanation of *how* a Highlight Report *is used*.

Tip 3. Start every question on a new piece of paper. This makes it much easier to add extra scribbles in the last few minutes of the exam.

Tip 4. In general you don't lose marks for saying something wrong, so don't cross things out. There are two exceptions to this:

- ❑ When you are asked to *list* relevant sub-processes and Products, ONLY list things that are relevant. If it's a 10 mark question find the 10 relevant items to go into the list and don't list anything else or marks will be taken away.

- ❑ When drawing Product Breakdown Structures and Product Flow Diagrams, marks are deducted for errors. (The PBS and PFD are very rules based diagrams – to maximise your marks learn the rules and then do not break them.)

Tip 5. There is no need to write a lot, or particularly well. Bullet points answers and brutally short ungrammatical partial sentences are fine as long as they answer the question and tell the examiner:

- ❑ which part of the method is relevant
- ❑ who is involved
- ❑ how it is used
- ❑ how it relates to the scenario.

The following fragment of an answer is acceptable Practitioner exam style. It minimises the words and maximises the marks:

"Project Board consist of:
Project Executive (Mrs Bigfish the CEO)
Owns Business Case
Ultimately responsible
Senior User (Fred Sellalot Marketing Manager)
Represents users of the new toaster
Senior Supplier (Head of Development Group)
Represents the design team and suppliers in the toaster project"

Tip 6.   The examiners are looking for certain PRINCE2 terms to be referenced and explained in each question. To get the marks you must state the correct term. For instance, using words like 'management' will not earn the mark reserved for referencing the term 'Project Board'.

Tip 7.   Perhaps 30% to 50% of the marks in an exam are awarded for referencing relevant terms. If you are not sure exactly what the question is looking for, spend 2 or 3 minutes brainstorming (on the answer paper!) a list of terms that you think *might* be relevant, and then spend the rest of the time writing about the terms from your list which you think are the ones needed. You will get a mark for any relevant PRINCE2 term that is in your brainstorm even if you did not go on to explain it. After you have answered all the questions in the exam come back to this question and explain a few more terms from your list. You won't lose marks for anything irrelevant. Don't worry about the order of your point making either. There are NO MARKS for 'a good read'. There are ONLY marks for relevant terms and relevant explanation and usage – any old order will do.

Tip 8.   You MUST relate your answers to the scenario if the question asks for it. This means quoting names of people, specific Products, situations, risks etc, rather than just providing pure method or general answers.

Tip 9.   There are a number of bits of the method that tend to get forgotten by Practitioner candidates in the pressure of the exam. Often the examiners will be looking for these terms to be referenced in your answers. You might lose out on 10 or so marks across the paper if you forget about:

> *Project Support, Lessons Learned Log and Report, End Project Report, Post Project Review, Follow-on Action Recommendations, Project Assurance from business AND user AND supplier perspectives.*

Tip 10. If you are unwell before the exam or excessively distressed tell the invigilator BEFORE the exam starts – they may be able to take this into account. If you have a physical disability, repetitive strain injury (RSI), dyslexia or similar personal challenge, make sure the APM Group and the Accredited Training Organisation know this a few weeks before the course and exam. Special arrangements may be applicable for you, however you have to give people time to arrange them.

The Timeline Fish

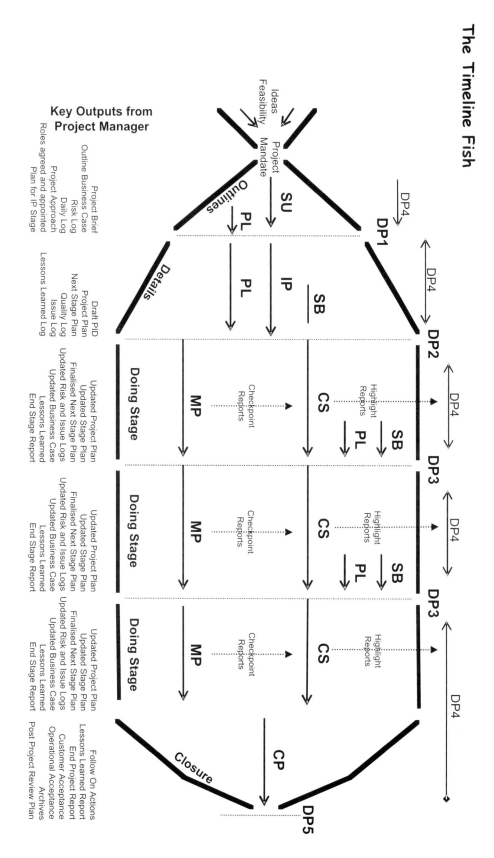

NOTES

NOTES